T0156693

GET YOUR
TRAVEL
On!

GET YOUR TRAVEL On!

FIVE KEYS TO PURSUING YOUR TRAVEL DREAMS

TARYN WHITE

Founder of *The Trip Wish List*

GET YOUR TRAVEL ON!
FIVE KEYS TO PURSUING YOUR TRAVEL DREAMS

Copyright © 2016 Taryn White.

All rights reserved. No part of this book may be used or reproduced by any means, graphic, electronic, or mechanical, including photocopying, recording, taping or by any information storage retrieval system without the written permission of the author except in the case of brief quotations embodied in critical articles and reviews.

iUniverse books may be ordered through booksellers or by contacting:

iUniverse
1663 Liberty Drive
Bloomington, IN 47403
www.iuniverse.com
1-800-Authors (1-800-288-4677)

Because of the dynamic nature of the Internet, any web addresses or links contained in this book may have changed since publication and may no longer be valid. The views expressed in this work are solely those of the author and do not necessarily reflect the views of the publisher, and the publisher hereby disclaims any responsibility for them.

Any people depicted in stock imagery provided by Thinkstock are models, and such images are being used for illustrative purposes only. Certain stock imagery © Thinkstock.

ISBN: 978-1-4917-9013-7 (sc)
ISBN: 978-1-4917-9014-4 (e)

Library of Congress Control Number: 2016902753

Print information available on the last page.

iUniverse rev. date: 06/14/2016

CONTENTS

To travel is to take a journey into yourself.
—Danny Kaye

INTRODUCTION

When you think of healthy living, I'm sure the common mantra advised by doctors comes to mind: eat right, exercise, and get plenty of sleep. But what if I told you there's a fourth aspect to health—taking regular vacations! That's right: everyone should take vacations annually for overall well-being. Not only does vacation allow you to eat right, exercise, and get plenty of sleep, but it also provides an additional element of relaxation and, oftentimes, broadens your horizons, both of which can be difficult to attain during your normal day-to-day life. When you take vacations, you're also doing things that you want to do and are able to spend continuous time engaging with people in a meaningful and personal way. That's why I make travel an integral part of my overall lifestyle. The ability to get away from it all and rejuvenate is a fundamental aspect of healthy living.

Unfortunately, in the United States, there is no mandatory vacation requirement allotted for workers, and this reality has spawned a workaholic culture in which many Americans are very reluctant to take time off for fear that doing so will negatively impact their careers. Living this way is detrimental not only to one's physical health but also to one's mental health. Study after study has shown that people who take regular vacations tend to live longer, some even cutting their risk of dying from a heart attack by as much as 50 percent, depending on the duration and frequency of vacationing. This risk sounds as bad as that of smoking. And if we contrast the no-vacation culture of the United States with that of other industrialized nations, it becomes very clear that the United States lags behind these countries, thereby lowering the quality of life and raising the incidence of illness.

It's often been said that time is money, but what good is more money if you can't translate it into the things you desire in life? Honestly, neither time nor money is a valid barrier to pursuing your travel dreams. The reason for this is that there are countless ways to see the world, and with travel credit cards and loyalty programs, you can earn massive amounts of miles and points in a matter of weeks, not years. You also don't need a lot of vacation time, as you can take incredible trips using the time you already have. The five key steps outlined in this book will help you develop a vision for travel, offer time-saving and proven tips to make travel easier, and provide strategies to help you travel the world for less money and less hassle. Step 1 will help you see travel in a new light, make it easier to pick a destination, and explain how to develop future plans for places that you'd like to visit. Step 2 demonstrates the concept of travel hacking, a methodology for securing high-value trips without the high cost so travel doesn't break the bank. Step 3 provides advice on what to pack and how to seamlessly fit your belongings into your suitcase without losing your mind, while step 4 provides an overview of buying travel insurance, because peace of mind and preparedness are important considerations when traveling. Lastly, step 5 is a comprehensive collection of travel tips that I've learned along the way from my experience visiting many corners of the world. The hope is that you develop a plan that, while requiring some effort, complements your lifestyle and motivates you to realize your travel dreams.

Step 1:

TRAVEL PLANNING

Adventure, however you define it, shouldn't be the appetizer of your life's experience; it should be the main course. And if your definition of adventure involves exploring the world, then pack your bags, because it's not as hard as it seems. All it takes is a little research, discipline, and planning—much like any other goal in life. I'm very much a planner and believe the mantra that writing down your goals will make them more concrete and achievable. In my experience, I've found that I am more likely to achieve a goal if I write it down and plan for it than if I don't. To that end, a few years ago, I created a travel plan, a detailed travel bucket list, since seeing the world has been my lifelong dream. There aren't many places I won't go, so my travel plan has me visiting nearly every country in the world during my lifetime. Even though I may not achieve this goal, I believe one should always dream big! Regardless, the mere thought of seeing the world drives me to continue my quests. Because of my travel goals, I have been able to visit all fifty US states and more than fifty countries, beginning with my must-see places in the short term and my like-to-see places in the long term. So how can you fulfill a lifelong dream of travel too? Well, just keep reading. The following sections will show you how I formulate my travel plans.

Fostering a Travel Mind-Set

Have you ever heard the phrase "Show me who your friends are, and I'll tell you who you are"? Well, those you surround yourself with make a

1

huge difference in pursuing any goal, including travel goals. My very first travel memory is that of a cross-country road trip to California with my family when I was only four years old. It was such an unforgettably long journey for my curious and impatient little self that I told my parents, "This ain't no vacation. All we're doing is driving." Of course, my family and I joke all the time about that experience, but you don't want to be around people who echo sentiments like my four-year-old self, so make an effort to reach out to friends and family members who support your desire to travel. Connecting with a community of people who share your passion for travel will provide encouragement to help you pursue your goals, and if your friends or family members are as serious about travel as you, they not only can help you foster a travel mind-set but also can become your travel companions. In addition, you and your travel companions can also become one another's accountability partners, which means that you hold each other accountable for making vacation a priority each year.

Other methods to foster a travel mind-set are to visit a destination from afar by reading travel content about that destination and by changing your perspective on travel from one where you simply export your activities and culture to a new destination to one where you embrace that which is different or unique, such as different customs and ways of thinking. Once I set a goal, I google the destination and read as much information as I can about that place over time, which provides background knowledge and furthers my interest in traveling there. Wikipedia is a wonderful resource for background information, especially on a country's history, demographics, and economy. Of course, you shouldn't exhaust yourself when traveling, because vacation should always be enjoyable. However, travel should not just be about relaxation; it should also be a quest for compelling experiences that result in your returning home a better you. Become an explorer and a learner first when traveling, because when you challenge yourself in this way, you can grow in ways that you never thought possible and gain a greater understanding of the world. And if you learn just one new thing about each place that you visit, you might discover a new way of doing things at home.

Picking a Destination

Picking a destination is one of the most exciting and motivating aspects of travel planning. Just daydreaming about relaxing on a Maldivian beach energizes me to travel now. So think about visiting your dream destination. If you've always dreamed of seeing the Eiffel Tower, go to Paris; or if architecture is your passion, why not visit Italy or Morocco? Without a doubt, visiting a dream destination will motivate you most and be most gratifying. Be very specific about your destinations (cities vs. countries), and don't sell your goals short, because you really can make it happen!

If you're having trouble deciding, make a list of things that you like to do or attractions you would like to visit. This list can include activities from surfing to shopping, or visiting monuments from the Parthenon to the Pantheon. To help you determine which destinations align with your interests, I created The Trip Wish List (www.tripwishlist.com), an online community where users can chart their travel bucket list aspirations and explore exciting activities and destinations.

If you still can't decide between a few places, you could opt to combine locations into a multidestination trip, many of which are easily booked online. One tip for creating multidestination trips is to build in stopovers at the connecting city. The connecting city is often the capital of the country, a great destination on its own. I usually take multidestination trips, because doing so allows me to see more destinations and increases the intrinsic value of my trip. In addition, when visiting multiple destinations, I always try to fly to the easternmost time zone first and work my way west, because once you get established in the foreign time zone, you gain "more" hours as you move westward. For example, 9:00 a.m. in one time zone is 8:00 a.m. in the time zone immediately to the west.

Don't skimp on trip planning and picking a destination, because setting a travel goal is very important, if not the most important part of the journey. However, before making any travel plans, you should first get a passport, if you don't already have one. Doing so will provide all the motivation to get your little blue book stamped. And if you have yet to travel abroad, the Caribbean, England, Canada, and Italy are great first-time destinations for Americans.

Weather and Seasons

The best time to visit a destination is a very important aspect of a trip that is often overlooked. Because the Northern and Southern Hemispheres have opposite seasons, it's always a great time to travel somewhere in the world. However, there are optimal times to visit certain destinations based on weather, price, and popularity. High season typically coincides with the Northern Hemisphere summer months of June through August, as well as a monthlong period around the Christmas and New Year's holidays. Low season is typically between mid-January and the end of March, and the shoulder seasons are typically the other months of the year, although these travel seasons can vary by destination.

Traveling during high season can be quite expensive, while low season can offer really cheap prices. However, during low season, some destinations shut down or are too hot for words (e.g., Greek islands during winter or the Middle East during summer), so visiting at this time means limited activity, bad weather, or both. The key to finding the best value (i.e., favorable weather, prices, and activities) is to arrive at the beginning or the end of peak or low season, because you will be able to score some really great travel bargains and avoid the crowds at some popular travel destinations. But there is absolutely nothing wrong with traveling during low or high season, as there are plenty of places to vacation.

The following are the best regions for travel during the four seasons of the year.

Best Winter Destinations

Excluding the weeks of Christmas and New Year's Day, December through February are great months to travel, with mid-January being particularly awesome as a result of decreased demand after the holiday travel period. Ideal destinations include the Caribbean (peak season owing to hurricanes in the summer), Central America, Southeast Asia, and Southern Africa. The North American Rockies and Alpine regions of Europe are popular ski destinations to visit during winter, and you can avoid peak prices in early December. If visiting Southeast Asia is on your wish list, winter is a terrific time to go, and there are many low-cost carriers that fly between countries, so if you find a cheap fare to one country, you may be able to visit another country for a marginal additional cost.

Best Spring Destinations

Springtime is perhaps my favorite time to travel, because the weather during this season is superb in most parts of the world. Europe is very appealing in spring because the weather is not as cold, flights are not as expensive, and crowds are not as large. Why not visit the gardens of Versailles or the canals of Venice? The Caribbean, Mexico, and Central America are also perfect to visit, because the Atlantic hurricane season has not yet begun and prices have dropped because of less demand from North American travelers. Spring is also an awesome time to visit the Southern Hemisphere destinations of South America (except during Carnival or Easter), the South Pacific (Australia, New Zealand, Oceania), and Southern Africa, because it's autumn in the Southern Hemisphere and the weather is generally wonderful, and in the South Pacific, you will avoid cyclone season, which runs from November through April. Hawaii is fabulous any time of the year, but during spring, you can avoid peak summer travel. The Middle East and North Africa are also great, because the immense hot weather is not in full effect. In Asia, it will be prior to typhoon season, so the weather will be fabulous. In East Africa, you can find deals on safaris—as well as avoid torrential rains during May and June, because these months follow the end of the heaviest rainy season, which runs from March through May.

Best Summer Destinations

Summer is definitely peak travel time, as there are so many people traveling around the world. It's summer break, and rates are high for traveling from North America to practically anywhere. In summer, though not off-peak, traveling to Canada and within the United States is superb. Alaska experiences its warmest weather, and there are a number of unique events there during the summer. The Caribbean, Central America, and Mexico offer the lowest rates of the year, but the weather is really hot and humid, and hurricane season is a factor. However, traveling prior to mid-July is usually just fine for these regions. East Africa is ideal to visit during summer, although prices for safaris increase drastically from July to September because the great annual wildlife migration heads from the Serengeti to the Maasai Mara during this period. Equatorial countries in South America are also good options.

Best Fall Destinations

Post–Labor Day is the perfect time to visit Hawaii and the national parks of the United States (the Grand Canyon, Yellowstone, Glacier National Park, etc.), because the weather is pleasant, rates have dropped, and the peak crowds have left. Similar to during the spring, it's also a wonderful time to visit the Southern Hemisphere: South America, the South Pacific, and Southern Africa. Europe is a bargain in the fall, as prices drop dramatically after October 1 and again after November 1. In addition, some southern European destinations, such as the Greek isles and southern Spain, still have sunny weather and tons of activities. Canada is beautiful this time of year, offering some fantastic fall foliage. The Middle East and North Africa are also fantastic because the hot and humid weather has lessened in the fall. India and South Asia are really awesome, as fall is after the monsoon season, which typically runs from late May through September. November and early December are typically good options for the Caribbean and Mexico, since hurricane season is winding down and it's not peak travel time.

Regardless of the season, you can visit practically any place at any time, so don't be discouraged if you can't visit a place during these recommended times of the year. You will have a great time wherever and whenever you go.

Developing Your Trip Wish List

Unless you're a digital nomad, self-employed, or retired, you probably have a specific number of vacation days, so traveling regularly for leisure requires developing a plan, and my first bit of advice is to visit The Trip Wish List and create your own travel bucket list of the top places you would like to visit. The more specific you can be, the better. I typically set goals for myself and backtrack to figure out the incremental steps to reach those goals, so if you have an idea where you would like to go, you can begin tailoring your activities toward this target. Much like exercise goals, dietary goals, or financial goals, travel goals can be easily segmented into daily, weekly, or monthly steps.

When I first started traveling, I began planning trips with a simple Excel spreadsheet. The elements of my planning included establishing a destination and a possible travel date, identifying a preliminary budget, figuring out a minimum monthly savings target, and factoring in any miles and points earned or to be attained in order to minimize costs. Estimates for meals, activities, and incidentals will depend on your chosen destination and duration. However, for a reasonable estimate, factor in $100 per person per day for meals and $25 per person per day for activities and incidentals.

Get Your Travel On **Simple Travel Planner**

	Short-Term (less than 2 years)
	Trip 1
Trip Goal	Paris, France
Trip Budget	$1,500
Monthly Savings Target	$200
Target Travel Date	June 20XX
Preferred Loyalty Program #1	Flying Blue
# of Miles and Points Required #1	100,000
Preferred Loyalty Program #2	Hyatt
# of Miles and Points Required #2	150,000

	Long-Term (2 to 5 years)		
	Trip 1	Trip 2	Trip 3
Trip Goal			
Trip Budget			
Monthly Savings Target			
Target Travel Date			
Preferred Loyalty Program #1			
# of Miles and Points Required #1			
Preferred Loyalty Program #2			
# of Miles and Points Required #2			

You don't have to create a long-term plan like me, but you should definitely have some ideas in the short term in order to maximize your vacation time and resources. My approach for each year has been to determine when and where I would like to travel, which can be based specifically on where I most want to go or on the best place to visit during the time frame I want to travel. Though usually a little more expensive, planning vacations around holidays is very practical, and once you determine when you will be able to take vacation, figure out the destinations from your list that align with the best seasons to travel.

Travel Research

So what websites should you use for travel research and to book trips? Well, that depends on what you seek. Once you have a trip idea, start your airfare search with the ITA Matrix (https://matrix.itasoftware.com) and Google Flights (http://www.google.com/flights). Among the many great features of the ITA Matrix is its advanced routing codes, which include searching by connecting city, airline alliance, and airline. I also use the ITA Matrix's one-way searches to see which airlines fly to which destinations and through which connecting cities; this is one way I determine many of my stopover destinations. Airline stopover rules, where allowable, can be found under the link to fare rules for your selected flight option within your ITA Matrix search results. While you cannot book flights directly on ITA Matrix, you can use the booking information on the site to book directly with the airlines. For more information on the ITA Matrix, Google has a great tutorial located at https://support.google.com/faqs/faq/1739451?hl=e.

Google Flights is another great website for airfare searches, and it can help you figure out when to go and even where to go. You can type in a region or country as the destination, or you can get inspired via its Discover Destinations application. When selecting "flexible dates", Google Flights displays a bar graph that allows you to browse real-time prices by calendar view, making it easy to find the lowest fare during a certain timeframe. Google Flights will also search segments separately, which could yield options that combine different services, such as an airline and an online travel agency, and Google Flights will suggest lower-price alternatives to your destination if applicable. Google has implemented a mobile-only travel search tool, Destinations on Google, which is accessible by adding the word "destinations" after the place you want to visit. Destinations on Google will provide cost comparisons, factoring in time of year and budget as well as provide recommended itineraries for exploring a destination. Given Google's track record, I'm sure this tool will only get better with time.

For hotel research, there are a number of worthy websites, but start your search with kayak.com (www.kayak.com) to compare pricing. If you're loyal to a particular hotel brand, the website of that brand is the best place to book rooms, because you will be able to earn points and obtain other benefits from your participation in the hotel's loyalty program. If you're more flexible on hotel options, check out sites like Rocketmiles (www.rocketmiles.com) and PointsHound (www.pointshound.com), which allow you to earn airline miles for paid hotel stays, as well as sites like Airbnb (www.airbnb.com), BedandBreakfast.com (www.bedandbreakfast.com), HomeAway (www.homeaway.com), VRBO (www.vrbo.com), and FlipKey (www.flipkey.com), because they often offer more affordable prices and are great options for families.

Most airfare search engines don't list budget carriers, such as Ryanair, so to perform flight searches for budget carriers, use WhichAirline (www.whichairline.com) or Skyscanner (www.skyscanner.net). FlyerTalk (www.flyertalk.com) and InsideFlyer (www.insideflyer.com) are the best online travel forums, where travelers discuss everything from miles and points to general travel. Search TripAdvisor (www.tripadvisor.com) to read hotel reviews and determine what specific hotels meet your standards. Generally, cleanliness, amenities, service quality, noise, cost, location, and inclusions, such as free Wi-Fi or breakfast, are the most important hotel considerations. In addition, watch recent videos of potential hotels on YouTube to get a more accurate depiction of the hotel rooms, facilities, and beaches, if applicable, because hotel website galleries sometimes don't provide the full scope.

Use SeatGuru (www.seatguru.com) or Skytrax (www.flatseats.com) to locate airplane seat maps and learn the best seats on an airplane. If the seat you wanted isn't available, you can sign up for Seat Alerts by ExpertFlyer (www.expertflyer.com), a free service that will notify you if and when your preferred seat becomes available. An easy seat hack when flying with a companion on an aircraft with a three-seat configuration is to not select the middle seat and select an aisle and a window seat on the same row. The reason for doing this is it's likely that another passenger will avoid selecting the middle seat, thus allowing you to have a row to yourselves. This hack doesn't always work, but you can always trade seats with a passenger who selects the middle seat.

While I am not endorsing any of these websites, the following websites are the 90 best websites for researching flight and accommodations options and travel deals.

Table 1: The 90 Best Sites for Travel Searches

Flights	Hotels	Accommodations	Travel Deals
Airfarewatchdog	Agoda	Airbnb	Daily Getaways
Booking Buddy	AllTheRooms	BedandBreakfast.com	Budget Travel
CheapAir	BidGoggles	Couchsurfing.com	CruiseDeals.com
CheapTickets	Booking.com	FlipKey	ExitFares
Dohop	DealBase	HomeExchange.com	Expedia
FareCompare	DreamCheaper	HomeAway	Fly4Free
Fly.com	Extreme Hotel Deals	Hostelbookers.com	Flyertalk
Google Flights	goSeek	Hostelz	Groupon Getaways
ITA Matrix	Hotel Quickly	Luxury Retreats	Hipmunk
Kayak	HotelTonight	MindMyHouse	lastminute.com
Low Cost Airlines	Hotels Combined	Rental Escapes	LivingSocial
Momondo	Hotels.com	Trampolinn	OneTravel
Skiplagged	Hotelwatchdog	Tripping.com	Orbitz
Skypicker	Hotwire	TrustedHousesitters.com	Secret Flying
Skyscanner	Innstant.com	Tug2.com	Smarter Travel
Tripdelta	Jetsetter	VacationRentals.com	The Fare Deal Alert
Vayama	PointsHound	Villas of Distinction	The Flight Deal
WhichAirline	RateDrop	VRBO	Tour Vacations To Go
Yapta	Rocketmiles	Wimdu	TravelPirates
	Room 77		Travelzoo
	Roomer		Travelocity
	Secret Escapes		TripAlertz
	Tingo		Tripdelta
	TravelPony		Vacations to Go
	Trivago		WebFlyer
	Voyage Privé		Yipit
	Wego		

Once you've applied these tips, you'll see that travel planning does not have to be overwhelming or complicated, and it really allows you to visualize your travel goals and make them more concrete. The five takeaways of step 1 are as follows:

- Surround yourself with people who support your passion for travel.
- Determine your travel interests and the activities you prefer.

- Create a trip wish list to chart your desired destinations, factoring in your travel dates, budget, and interests.
- Use the 90 best sites to assist with travel research, beginning with the ITA Matrix for flights.
- Consider the season and weather when picking a destination and making trip reservations.

Step 2:

TRAVEL HACKING

Travel hacking is the art of securing extremely discounted travel, and it's more than just finding a deal; it's a methodology to maximize your spending and your redemptions for travel that might otherwise not be attainable. The basis of travel hacking is obtaining travel rewards points through travel loyalty programs and travel credit cards without having to do a lot of traveling. An example of travel hacking would be obtaining 320,000 United Airlines miles solely through various travel credit cards to book two business-class flights to Asia, which retail for $4,000 per person. In order to successfully travel hack, it's important to

- have good credit,
- be diligent about credit card spending, and
- have a travel goal in mind.

The content in this section of the book is for educational purposes only and should not be construed as professional financial advice. Before continuing in this section, it would be worthwhile to visit the glossary in order to review definitions of key travel-hacking concepts.

In its simplest form, hacking your trip involves four steps:

1. Pick a destination from your trip wish list that you would like to visit.
2. Have a budget for your trip in mind.

3. Determine which flight and hotel options for your chosen destination exist for the least cost, either in money, miles, or points.
4. Obtain sufficient loyalty and reward points via a targeted approach in order to book low-cost flights, hotels, and other trip items.

Websites that can assist you with understanding how many miles and points you need and the cheapest mileage redemption options are Award Ace (www.awardace.com), Milez.biz (www.milez.biz), AwardMapper (www.awardmapper.com), FlyerMiler (www.flyermiler.com), Award-o-matic (www.awardomatic.com), and Wandering Aramean (www.wandr.me). You must determine which hotel options at your chosen destination offer the best value and meet your standards. Keep in mind that best value does not mean budget hotels; you can stay in five-star accommodations for a fraction of the advertised price. For more specific details on how to earn loyalty points, visit the section "Earning Miles and Points," which follows.

Loyalty Programs

Practically every company now has a loyalty program, which is simply a rewards program that offers benefits to frequent customers. In theory, the more purchases you make, the more benefits or status you receive. The overall goal of travel loyalty programs is to accrue points for discounted travel, with elite status being a nice perk. Therefore, it is important to understand airline alliances as well as airline and hotel programs in general. An overview of airline alliances, airline routes, and top airline programs is located in the following subsections, and an overview of hotel loyalty programs is located in appendix B.

Airline Alliances

When planning where to go and which airline to choose, you should familiarize yourself with the three major airline alliances to learn which airlines fly where. Most international airlines belong to one of these three airline alliances: oneworld, SkyTeam, and Star Alliance. These alliances enable travelers to access a variety of destinations via partnerships and flight codeshares. Below are the airline alliance member airlines and the non-alliance partners of the three major US legacy carriers: American Airlines, Delta Airlines, and United Airlines.

Oneworld
Air Berlin
American Airlines
British Airways
Cathay Pacific
Finn Air
Iberia
Japan Airlines
LATAM
Malaysia Airlines
Qantas
Qatar Airways
Royal Jordanian
S7 Airlines
Sri Lankan Airlines

American Partners
Air Tahiti Nui
Alaska Airlines
Cape Air
EL AL
Etihad
Fiji Airlines
Hainan Airlines
Hawaiian Airlines
Jet Airways
Jetstar
Seabourne
WestJet

SkyTeam
Aeroflot
Aerolineas Argentina
Aeromexico
Air Europa
Air France
Alitalia
China Airlines
China Eastern
China Southern
Czech Airlines
Delta Airlines
Garuda Indonesia
Kenya Airways
KLM
Korean Air
Middle East Airlines
Saudia Airlines
Tarom Airlines
Vietnam Airlines
Xiamen Air

Delta Partners
Alaska
GOL
Hawaiian Airlines
Olympic Air
Virgin Atlantic
Virgin Australia
WestJet

Star Alliance
Adria Airlines
Aegean Airlines
Air Canada
Air China
Air India
Air New Zealand
ANA
Asiana Airlines
Austrian
Avianca/TACA
Brussels Airlines
Copa Airlines
Croatia Airlines
EgyptAir
Ethiopian Airlines
Eva Air
LOT Polish Airlines
Lufthansa
Scandinavian Airlines
Shenzhen Airlines
Singapore Airlines
South African Airways
SWISS
TAP Portugal
Thai Airways
Turkish Airlines
United Airlines

United Partners
Aer Lingus
Aeromar
Air Dolomiti
Azul
Cape Air
Edelweiss
Germanwings
Great Lakes Airlines
Hawaiian Airlines
Island Air
Jet Airways
Silver Airways

Even though each alliance serves every region, each of the three airline alliances has a particularly good variety of routes and/or carriers for the following regions (regions are not as defined by airline alliances):

Region	oneworld	SkyTeam	Star Alliance
Africa			✓
Asia	✓	✓	✓
Caribbean	✓		
Central America	✓		✓
Europe	✓	✓	✓
Middle East	✓		
North America	✓	✓	✓
South America	✓		✓
South Pacific	✓	✓	✓

The greatest benefit of airline partnerships is access to more routes and destinations than a single carrier can afford to provide. An additional benefit is that you don't have to always fly on US-based carriers but can still credit miles flown to your US-based airline's frequent flyer account. This benefit will become increasingly more attractive if airlines continue to devalue their loyalty programs by increasing award redemption rates. When redeeming miles from your US-based airline on foreign carriers, you do not actually transfer the miles from the US-based airline to the foreign airline but use the US-based airline's miles to redeem flights on the foreign carrier. Many foreign carriers participate in transferrable-points programs, such as American Express Membership Rewards, in which points can be directly transferred into your foreign airline's loyalty program account. In this case, you would follow the foreign carrier's rules and award chart. Since most foreign partner airlines levy heavy fuel surcharges for flights outside the Americas, it is very important to consider this cost when booking flights on foreign carriers. Even when fuel prices are relatively inexpensive, airlines have continued to pass on fuel surcharges to consumers. Owing to a US Department of Transportation regulation stipulating that fuel surcharges be tied to fuel prices, airlines have renamed this fee "carrier-imposed charges" or "YQ surcharge" in an effort to avoid the regulations. Major airlines that do not impose fuel surcharges on any award flights are Avianca/TACA, JetBlue, LATAM [LAN and TAM], Southwest, and United.

Currently, there are ten major US-based airlines: Alaska, American, Delta, Frontier, Hawaiian, JetBlue, Southwest, Spirit, United, and Virgin America. As mergers have taken place over the years, the number of US-based airlines has decreased, which has had a great impact on ticket prices and airline loyalty program benefits. In the past, US Airways, Continental Airlines, and United belonged to Star Alliance, which meant that award redemption options were plentiful and devaluations were minimal. Nowadays, US-based airlines have a virtual monopoly on US flyers, particularly within the three airline alliances, and one can only wonder what the future holds for airline loyalty programs. Despite these changes, you can extract incredible value by using rewards points. So, while some rules have changed, the game remains the same.

For comparisons between airline programs, Bankrate (www.bankrate.com) publishes an excellent online tool for US-based airlines, including fees and seat comparisons, while WanderBat (www.wanderbat.com) provides similar information for numerous international airline programs.

Airline Routes

To determine which airlines fly where, and before booking any flights, you should review airline alliance route maps. Since no one airline website contains all award availability, it's best to check multiple sources. For the best award-seat-availability searches, use Qantas and British Airways for oneworld, Flying Blue for SkyTeam, and Air Canada, ANA, and United for Star Alliance. For a more comprehensive service, ExpertFlyer and the KVS Availability Tool offer extensive award availability searches as well as seat alerts as a paid service.

Another great resource for learning which airlines fly where is Wikipedia's Airlines and Destinations sections, which provide a listing of airlines that fly into specific airports and the destinations to which those airlines fly from the specified airport. The easiest way to find this airport-specific information in Wikipedia is to type the name of the city and the words "international airport" in the search bar on Wikipedia's home page.

Once you have a better understanding of the possible routings to your destination, search for award availability on your chosen carrier and within your chosen alliance, if applicable. This often means searching individual airline websites, including those of partner airlines.

Top Airlines for Award Flights

When considering which airlines to choose for award flights, you should not limit your options to US-based carriers, as there are both domestic and foreign airlines from which to choose. Below is a brief overview of the best airlines with which to redeem miles for award flights. Since this information is subject to change, you should always visit each airline's website for the most up-to-date information.

Alaska Airlines (www.alaskaair.com)

Alaska Airlines does not belong to an alliance but has a great list of partner airlines that include alliance and non-alliance airlines. One great use of Alaska Airlines Mileage Plan miles is the ability to book a stopover on a one-way international award ticket. You can obtain Alaska Airlines Mileage Plan miles through flights on Alaska Airlines and partner airlines, Starwood American Express transfers, Diners Club International transfers, and the Alaska Airlines Bank of America cobranded credit card.

Al Nippon Airways (ANA) (www.ana.co.jp/asw/wws/us/e/)

One of the national airlines of Japan, ANA's loyalty program is a region-based program with some of the cheapest redemption rates among all airline programs. For example, award flights from the United States to Europe are 55,000 miles in economy and 88,000 miles in business class. However, ANA imposes expensive fuel surcharges on some flights, and connections will only add to the fees and taxes. ANA has non–Star Alliance partners, which include Etihad, Garuda Indonesia, Hawaiian, Jet Airways, TAM, and Virgin Atlantic, but you can't combine flights on these additional partners like you can on Star Alliance awards. A really great redemption using ANA is its around-the-world award ticket, because ANA allows up to eight stopovers for 65,000 miles in economy and 105,000 miles in business class.

American Airlines (www.aa.com)

A member of the oneworld Alliance, American Airlines has the most extensive network to the Caribbean. Unfortunately, most American Airlines partner award flights are not bookable online and must be booked via phone. Like some other airlines, American Airlines converted to a revenue-based mileage-earning structure. One best use of American Airlines AAdvantage miles is for off-peak (discounted) award tickets to Hawaii, Europe, South America, and Asia. Stopovers are not allowed, but one-way awards are allowed. You can obtain American Airlines AAdvantage miles through flights on American Airlines, oneworld airlines, and partner airlines; Starwood American Express transfers; and American Airlines Citi co-branded credit cards.

British Airways (www.ba.com)

British Airways has a distance-based program and is the best airline program for short-distance award flights across the world. For example, British Airways charges as little as 4,000 miles one-way for flights of 650 miles or less, although that rate can no longer be redeemed for flights from the United States. One of the downsides of British Airways is very high fuel surcharges on certain carriers. Fuel surcharges can be avoided by flying within the Americas or by flying on Air Berlin, Aer Lingus, or Alaska Airlines. In addition to earning through airline partners and co-branded credit cards, British Airways has the following transfer partners: American Express Membership Rewards, Starwood American Express, Diners Club International, and Chase Ultimate Rewards.

Cathay Pacific (www.cathaypacific.com)

Cathay Pacific's Asia Miles program is a distance-based loyalty program allowing five stops and two open-jaws on a round-trip award. As with most foreign carriers, fuel surcharges tend to be high on Cathay Pacific flights, so flying within the Americas or flying on Air Berlin, Aer Lingus, or Alaska Airlines generally avoids fuel surcharges. From the eastern United States to Europe costs 60,000 miles in economy and 80,000 miles in business class, which is a great deal if you avoid the fuel surcharges. Asia Miles is a transfer partner of American Express Membership Rewards and Starwood American Express.

Delta Airlines (www.delta.com)

Though SkyTeam member Delta has improved its notoriously bad website, booking awards remains a significant trial-and-error process, as trying to figure out the pricing of different awards is virtually impossible—pun intended. Because of this difficulty, I recommend booking Delta awards only for partner flights, such as Virgin Australia and Virgin Atlantic. As such, booking SkyTeam award flights should first be pursued with Flying Blue (the loyalty program of Air France and KLM), which often offers Delta flights for fewer miles. Delta allows one-way awards but not stopovers and open-jaw flights. You can obtain Delta Airlines SkyMiles through flights on Delta, SkyTeam Airlines, and partner airlines; Starwood American Express transfers; American Express Membership Rewards transfers; Diners Club International transfers; and Delta American Express co-branded credit cards.

Flying Blue (www.flyingblue.com)

Flying Blue is the airline loyalty program for Air France and KLM and a transfer partner of American Express Membership Rewards, Citi ThankYou Points, and Starwood American Express. Flying Blue allows one stopover and one open-jaw on round-trip awards, but stopovers cannot be booked online. One of the best uses of Flying Blue is its Promo Awards, in which the miles required for certain routes are discounted 50 percent for a limited time. However, these discounted Promo Awards usually have much higher taxes and fees than regular awards on Flying Blue. Some of the best redemptions using Flying Blue miles are the United States to Europe for 50,000 miles in economy, the United States to Hawaii for 30,000 miles in economy, and the United States to Tahiti for 60,000 miles round-trip in economy.

Korean Airlines (www.koreanair.com)

Korean Airlines, a SkyTeam partner airline is one of the national airlines of South Korea and a transfer partner of Chase Ultimate Rewards, Diners Club International, and Starwood American Express. The airline's SKYPASS loyalty program allows one stopover and one open-jaw flight on awards on partner airlines. Fuel surcharges are often levied with this program, and this program requires round-trip award booking if using partner airlines. The best redemptions using this program are 25,000 miles round-trip to Hawaii in economy, 50,000 miles round-trip from the United States to Europe in economy and 80,000 in business class, and 60,000 miles round-trip to Tahiti in economy and 90,000 miles in business class.

Lufthansa (www.lufthansa.com)

Lufthansa is the national airline of Germany and a transfer partner of Starwood American Express. While it has high fuel surcharges, it offers great award flight options. For example, the airline allows two stopovers on award tickets (one stopover in each direction). In addition, Lufthansa considers all of South America to be one region; the Caribbean and Central America are treated as one region as well. This means that flying from the United States to South America, Central America, and the Caribbean are fantastic options to consider, because you could stop over in one destination in South America en route to another destination in South America. However, you could not stop over in the Caribbean / Central America region while flying from South America without an increase in the miles required.

Singapore Airlines (www.singaporeair.com)

Singapore Airlines, a Star Alliance partner airline, is a transfer partner of American Express Membership Rewards, Chase Ultimate Rewards, Citi ThankYou, and Starwood American Express. Singapore Airlines' KrisFlyer loyalty program is distance-based and has two award charts— one for Singapore and Silk Air, and one for partner airlines. For partner awards, Singapore allows one stopover and one open-jaw with up to three additional stopovers costing $100 each (some restrictions apply) for partner awards. Round-trip award flights to Hawaii cost 35,000 miles in economy, 60,000 miles in business, and 80,000 miles in first class, while round-trip award flights to Europe cost 55,000 miles in economy, 130,000 miles in business, and 160,000 miles in first class. Awards on partner airlines must be booked by calling Singapore Airlines, and there is no telephone booking fee. When booking award flights online on Singapore Airlines and Silk Air, there is a 15 percent discount in miles, and this mileage discount is great for booking the highly coveted Singapore Suites (Airbus 380), for which Singapore Airlines releases availability only to Singapore's KrisFlyer members.

Southwest Airlines (www.southwest.com)

Southwest Airlines, a low-cost US carrier, is unique in that it does not charge baggage or change fees. The Southwest Companion Pass is one of the most lucrative travel products on the market, because if you have the Companion Pass, your companion flies free on every flight, including flights booked using Rapid Rewards points. To obtain the Companion Pass, you must either fly 100 one-way qualifying flights or earn 110,000 Southwest points in a calendar year. Earning 110,000 points can be easily achieved by applying for Southwest's personal and business credit cards, which each provide up to 50,000 points after meeting minimum spending requirements. Southwest Rapid Rewards miles can be obtained on Southwest flights, through Chase Ultimate Rewards transfers, through Diners Club International transfers, and through Southwest Airlines Rapid Rewards credit cards. Southwest frequently offers fare deals through its Click 'n Save specials.

United Airlines (www.united.com)

United Airlines is one of the three remaining US legacy carriers (along with American and Delta). Similar to Delta, United has converted from an earning structure based on miles flown to one based on dollars spent, but miles flown on United partners, depending on the partner and fare class, will still earn miles based on miles flown when being credited to your MileagePlus account. United has two separate award charts for United awards and partner airline awards, in which the partner award chart has higher pricing for premium cabin awards. One of the best attributes of United's loyalty program is the ability to book open-jaw flights and stopovers, as well as to use United Airlines miles to book intraregional flights (e.g., flights within Oceania and the Caribbean). MileagePlus miles can be earned through United Airlines, Star Alliance airline, and partner airline flights; Chase Ultimate Rewards transfers; and United Airlines Chase co-branded credit cards.

Qualifying for Elite Status

Silver, gold, platinum, and diamond—sounds like a jewelry store, doesn't it? Well, these precious materials are often used to describe one of the key benefits of airline and hotel loyalty programs: elite status. With airline and hotel loyalty programs, elite status can be very valuable, elevating your travel experience with complimentary added benefits that include free Wi-Fi, priority check-in, priority airport screening, waived fees, free checked baggage, extra baggage allowances, lounge access, and free breakfasts. And status is one of the best ways to maximize your points, because it also provides higher earning bonuses for spending, flights, and stays. Some hotel co-branded credit cards offer elite status or stay credits toward elite status for having an account. In order to earn points from stays with hotel brands, you must book directly with the hotel and not with consolidator sites, such as hotels.com.

Though elite status can be very useful, it is not a must-have item or prerequisite for travel or for membership in loyalty programs. Therefore, before seeking elite status, it's important to evaluate whether it will be beneficial for you, because if you pursue elite status via credit cards, there are costs involved in the form of credit card annual fees and spending requirements. However, the benefits of credit cards usually go well beyond simply obtaining elite status (e.g., Global Entry, statement credits, etc.). It's worth noting that you do not need elite airline status if flying in premium class, because doing so gives you many of the perks of elite status. In addition, for most hotel programs, having certain credit cards will give you at least the lowest tier of elite status, and you can usually spend your way to the top.

In some cases, if you earn top-tier status with one loyalty program, another loyalty program will match your status. One such example is RewardsPlus, which offers United Gold, Platinum, or 1K members automatic Gold Elite status with Marriott Rewards. This is a great benefit because, except for airlines that operate under a revenue-based earning structure, top-tier airline status typically requires earning more than 100,000 elite qualifying miles annually. At the end of the calendar year, if you have not met the eligibility requirements to maintain elite status, you might need to do a mileage or mattress run, which involves booking cheap flights or cheap hotel rooms for the purpose of earning enough qualifying points or qualifying stays to achieve elite status.

Airline Elite Status

Generally, airline elite status can be obtained via earning a specific number of elite qualifying miles, which is the number of miles credited from a paid flight and is typically based on miles flown, or earning a specific number of elite qualifying segments, which is based on the number of flights (e.g., JFK–ATL is one segment). The following list provides the criteria for earning elite status with the three US legacy airlines and the mileage bonuses associated with each elite tier. This information is subject to change, as a result of the fluidity of travel loyalty program benefits.

American Airlines
Elite Status Tiers
- Gold—25,000 Elite Qualifying Miles (EQM) or 30 segments; mileage benefit = 25% mileage bonus
- Platinum—50,000 EQM or 6 segments; mileage benefit = 100% mileage bonus
- Executive Platinum—100,000 EQM or 120 segments; mileage benefit = 100% mileage bonus

The Citi Executive AAdvantage World Elite MasterCard allows you to earn up to 10,000 EQM after spending $40,000. The card has a $450 annual fee.

Delta
Elite Status Tiers
- Silver—25,000 Medallion Qualification Miles (MQM) and $3,000; mileage benefit = 25% mileage bonus

- Gold—50,000 MQM and $6,000; mileage benefit = 100% mileage bonus
- Platinum—75,000 MQM and $9,000; mileage benefit = 100% mileage bonus
- Diamond—125,000 MQM and $15,000; mileage benefit = 125% mileage bonus

With both Delta co-branded American Express cards, the Delta Reserve ($450 annual fee) and Platinum Delta SkyMiles ($150 annual fee) credit cards, you could earn up to 60,000 MQM, but doing so requires a ton of spending, and given Delta's numerous devaluations, I'm not sure it's a good decision unless you're a frequent Delta traveler. Delta does allow you to roll over MQMs beyond your qualification tier for the next year's status, and it also has the Choice Benefits program, which allows Platinum and Diamond members to gift Silver or Gold status, respectively, to someone else.

United
Elite Status Tiers
- Silver—25,000 Premier Qualifying Miles (PQM) or 30 segments and $2,500; mileage benefit = 25% mileage bonus
- Gold—50,000 PQM or 60 segments and $5,000; mileage benefit = 50% mileage bonus
- Platinum—75,000 PQM or 90 segments and $7,500; mileage benefit = 75% mileage bonus
- 1K—100,000 PQM and $10,000; mileage benefit = 100% mileage bonus
- Global Services—invitation only

Currently, United does not offer a credit card that earns PQM.

Hotel Elite Status

The easiest way to gain hotel elite status is via co-branded credit cards, whether you travel frequently or not, because many loyalty programs offer elite status for simply having their credit card. Others give you stay or night credits toward elite status for having their credit card. These cards provide points per dollar spent that are in addition to the points earned from paid stays as a member of the program. Even though most of these cards come with annual fees, the benefits of the cards (i.e., free breakfasts) usually outweigh the annual fees, and you should check to see if the annual fee is waived for the first year. Also, some hotel programs have top-tier promotional programs in which you can earn top-tier status for completing a number of nights during a specified time frame. For example, Hyatt offers base members Platinum status for completing six nights during a sixty-day trial period and Diamond status for completing twelve nights during the same sixty-day trial period. The following information provides an overview of hotel elite status requirements for US-based hotel programs. As a result, it excludes Fairmont hotels, a very popular Canadian-based hotel chain that should also be considered for award stays, elite status, and its co-branded credit card. This information is subject to change as a result of the fluidity of travel loyalty program benefits.

Best Western
Elite Status Tiers
- Gold—10 nights or 10,000 base points; points bonus: 10% bonus
- Platinum—15 nights or 15,000 base points; points bonus: 15% bonus
- Diamond—30 nights or 30,000 base points; points bonus: 30% bonus

The Best Western Rewards MasterCard offers automatic Gold status, and the Best Western Rewards Business MasterCard and Best Western Rewards Premium MasterCard offer automatic Platinum status.

Choice
Elite Status Tiers
- Gold—10 nights; points bonus: 10% bonus
- Platinum—20 nights; points bonus: 25% bonus
- Diamond—40 nights; points bonus: 50% bonus

The Choice Privileges Visa Signature card offers automatic Gold Elite status.

Club Carlson
Elite Status Tiers
- Silver—15 nights or 10 stays; points bonus: 15% bonus
- Gold—35 nights or 20 stays; points bonus: 35% bonus
- Concierge—75 nights or 30 stays; points bonus: 75% bonus

The Club Carlson Premier Rewards Visa Signature and Club Carlson Business Rewards Visa offer automatic Gold status, while the Club Carlson Rewards Visa offers automatic Silver status.

Hilton HHonors
Elite Status Tiers

- Silver—10 nights or 4 stays; points bonus: 15% bonus
- Gold—40 nights, 20 stays, or 75,000 base points; points bonus: 25% bonus
- Diamond—60 nights, 30 stays, or 120,000 base points; points bonus: 50% bonus

The Citi Hilton HHonors Visa Signature and Hilton HHonors American Express cards offer automatic Silver status. The Citi Hilton HHonors Reserve and Hilton HHonors Surpass American Express cards offer automatic Gold status, and Platinum status if you spend $40,000 on one of these two cards within a calendar year.

Hyatt Gold Passport
Elite Status Tiers
- Gold—membership level for enrollment; points bonus: 5 points per dollar spent at Hyatt properties

- Platinum—15 nights or 5 stays; points bonus: 15% bonus
- Diamond—50 nights or 25 stays; points bonus: 30% bonus

The Hyatt Visa credit card offers automatic Platinum status.

IHG Rewards
Elite Status Tiers
- Gold—15 nights, 20,000 Elite Qualifying Points (EQP), or Fast Track by staying 10 nights at 3 IHG brands; points bonus: 10% bonus
- Platinum—50 nights, 60,000 EQP, or Fast Track by staying 40 nights at 4 IHG brands; points bonus: 50%
- Spire—75 nights or 75,000 EQP; points bonus: 100% bonus

The IHG Rewards Club Select MasterCard offers automatic Platinum status. You can obtain InterContinental Ambassador status for $200 or 32,000 points, but if you don't have at least Gold status, you will be upgraded only to Gold status, not Ambassador status. InterContinental Royal Ambassador status, the highest tier within IHG, is by invitation only. Ambassador status is only applicable at InterContinental properties.

Marriott/Ritz-Carlton Rewards
Elite Status Tiers
- Silver—10 nights; points bonus: 20% bonus
- Gold—50 nights; points bonus: 25% bonus
- Platinum—75 nights; points bonus: 50% bonus

The Marriott Rewards, Rewards Premier, and Rewards Premier Business Visa credit cards offer automatic Silver status due to a fifteen-night credit toward elite status annually.

Starwood Preferred Guest
Elite Status Tiers
- Gold—25 nights or 10 stays; points bonus: 3 Starpoints for every dollar spent on eligible stays
- Platinum—50 nights or 25 stays; points bonus: 3 Starpoints for every dollar spent on eligible stays

The Starwood Preferred Guest and Preferred Guest Business American Express cards offer five nights and two stays toward elite status annually or Gold status after spending $30,000 in eligible purchases in a calendar year. The American Express Platinum card offers automatic Gold status.

Wyndham
Elite Status Tiers
- Gold—20 nights; points bonus: 10 points per dollar spent on eligible stays; 15,000 Gold status points that can be redeemed for a Go Free or Go Fast award.

Currently, Wyndham does not have a credit card that offers elite status.

Earning Miles and Points

The first step in any personal travel strategy should be to focus on spending, and the single greatest piece of advice I can offer you is to put all of your spending on points-earning or cash-back credit cards and pay the full balances within thirty days. Simply put, all shopping should earn either travel rewards points, cash back, or both. Not only does this practice protect your bank accounts from potential data breaches from using your bank debit card, but it also rewards you for purchases you already make. Again, even though some travel cards have annual fees, the benefits of those cards outweigh the annual fees in most cases. It is important to pay your credit card balances in full each month, because carrying credit card debt is not a good strategy. You should also not obtain credit cards if you are not good with debt management.

Spending Strategies to Earn Miles and Points

Travel credit cards have three primary groupings: transferable, fixed value, and co-branded. The fourth type of credit card, cash-back credit cards, is not limited to travel but can be effective for saving for travel. These four terms are further defined in the glossary. Some examples of the credit card groupings are below:

1. Transferable: American Express, Chase, Diners Club, Starwood American Express (Starwood is both transferrable and co-branded).

2. Fixed value: Barclay Arrival Plus, Capital One
3. Co-branded: Marriott, Hilton, Hyatt, IHG, Delta, United, American, Amtrak
4. Cash back: American Express, Discover, Capital One, Chase, US Bank

When using travel credit cards, you will typically earn 1 point for every dollar spent in regular purchases, while earning multiple points per dollar spent in certain categories, such as airfare, dining, groceries, gas, restaurants, travel, and office supply stores. If you book airfare through American Express Travel and you have a Membership Rewards credit card, you will earn an additional point per dollar spent, which equates to four points per dollar spent. Chase Ultimate Rewards also offers an additional point for booking travel through its site. However, American Express Travel and Chase Ultimate Rewards typically do not offer the lowest rates, so you have to decide if the extra point per dollar spent is worth the extra dollars spent. If the prices are comparable, you should book within the American Express or Chase portals, but if prices are not, it is usually not worth the extra cost. In addition, American Express Travel charges up to $11 for booking flights through its site.

Cash-back cards can be very useful if you can earn at least 5 percent cash back on every dollar spent, but most cash-back cards earn around 1 percent per dollar spent for general purchases. However, the Discover it credit card offers double cash back during your first year of membership, effectively doubling your efforts. With most other cash-back cards, to make the cash-back approach work, you would need to have multiple cash-back cards and use them where you can maximize category bonus spending. For example, the American Express Blue Cash Preferred card earns 6 percent cash back at supermarkets (up to $6,000 per year in purchases), but this limit doesn't preclude you from having more than one card. So if you had $20,000 in total annual spending via multiple cards at 6 percent cash back, you could earn $1,200 cash back annually, but it would take a lot of effort because most cash-back credit cards have different bonus spending categories and usually have caps on how much cash back you can earn in bonus spending categories. Nonetheless, cash-back credit cards might be the future of travel and rewards credit cards, given the continuous cycle of airline and hotel loyalty program devaluations.

So which credit cards should you have in your wallet? At a minimum, you should have at least one travel credit card, and ideally, you should have a mix of credit cards. This will allow you to maximize your points earning from spending in a variety of categories and diversify your portfolio of points so you will be able to redeem them from a variety of programs that suit your needs. The following cards represent three of the best credit cards for travel.

- <u>American Express Premier Rewards Gold:</u> This card earns 3 points per dollar spent with airlines; 2 points at US restaurants, US gas stations, and US supermarkets; and 1 point on all other purchases. The card has no foreign transaction fees, a $100 airline fee credit, and a $195 annual fee, which is waived during the first year of card membership. The sign-up bonus is 25,000 points after spending $2,000 within the first three months of card membership. American Express Membership Rewards has twenty transfer partners, including Hilton, Delta, JetBlue, and Flying Blue.
- <u>Chase Sapphire Preferred:</u> This card earns 2 points for travel and dining at restaurants and 1 point for all other purchases. The card has no foreign transaction fees and an annual fee of $95, which is waived during the first year of card membership. The sign-up bonus for the card is 50,000 points after spending $4,000 within the first three months of card membership. The 2 points on all travel is a fantastic option, because travel spending tends to represent large expenditures, so you can rack up the points quickly when you use this card on vacation. Chase Ultimate Rewards has ten transfer partners, including United, Marriott, Hyatt, and Southwest Airlines.
- <u>Starwood American Express:</u> This card earns 1 point per dollar spent and has a sign-up bonus of 25,000 points after spending $3,000 during the first three months of card membership. The card has an annual fee of $65, which is waived during the first year of card membership. The best benefit of this card is that it acts like a transferable points program, allowing you to transfer

miles to more than thirty airlines (more than any other program). In addition, you receive a 5,000-point transfer bonus for every 20,000 points you transfer to airlines.

Other noteworthy cards to consider are the Barclay Arrival Plus, a fixed-value card that earns 2 points per dollar spent, offers a 40,000-point sign-up bonus, and waives the eighty-nine-dollar annual fee during the first year; the Citi Double Cash Back card, a no-annual-fee card that earns 2 percent cash back on all purchases with no annual caps and restrictions; the Discover it card, a no-annual-fee card that earns between 1 percent and 5 percent cash back and doubles the cash back earned during the first year of card membership; the Citi Prestige MasterCard, a transferable-points card that offers a 50,000 sign-up bonus after spending $3,000 in three months, earns 3 points per dollar spent on air travel and hotels and 2 points per dollar spent on dining and entertainment, and provides the option for a fourth night free at any hotel; and the Citi AAdvantage Platinum Select MasterCard, which offers 10 percent of your miles back when redeemed for awards and is one of the few ways to earn American Airlines AAdvantage miles without flying. There are a plethora of other great cards on the market, with new ones popping up every year, and a useful site for finding the best credit card offers is the CardMatch tool offered by CreditCards.com.

Applying for Travel Credit Cards

The key to applying for travel credit cards is to target those that have high sign-up bonuses and minimal fees and to have an aspirational goal for which you want to use the miles. This will help you determine which cards to obtain. If you're planning to apply for multiple cards, it's best to apply for multiple cards on the same day so that creditors don't see numerous credit inquiries on your report, or to apply in ninety-day intervals, since credit inquires have less impact over time. In addition, if you're able to document a business need, you can apply for both personal and business credit cards, thereby doubling your sign-up bonus points. The beauty of doing so is that points accrued from both credit cards can be linked to the same loyalty program account, and the business credit card spending does not show up on your personal credit report.

If you plan to cancel a card before the annual fee is due, make sure that you either liquidate or transfer the rewards points to another account, either with that credit card company or a transfer partner. Otherwise you will lose the points you earned, because your points are linked to your credit card account. Canceling co-branded airline and hotel credit cards will not affect the points you have earned, because your points are linked to your loyalty program account, not a credit card account. Before canceling a card, you should ask for a waiver of the annual fee or for bonus miles for keeping the card. You should also inquire about downgrading to a card without annual fees to keep the credit line open.

Manufactured Spending

Manufactured spending is like regular credit card spending on steroids because the volume of spending and credit card balances are artificially enhanced in order to accrue miles and points. However, manufactured spending enables you to earn rewards points without incurring more spending because you either use your travel credit cards to pay for regular expenses, including mortgages and student loans, or to purchase "nothing" for the purpose of earning rewards points. If you're new to manufactured spending or new to a particular method, start small to determine your level of comfort.

The fastest way to accrue miles and points is via credit card sign-up bonuses and churning, which is the practice of continually closing accounts and reapplying for rewards credit cards for the sole purpose of attaining sign-up bonuses. You might be wondering if churning harms your credit score. Well, new credit inquiries represent only 10 percent of your credit score, with type of credit, payment history, credit history, and utilization representing the remaining 90 percent of your score. This means that while new credit inquiries will cause a dip in your score in the short term, by opening a new account you can actually improve your utilization ratios because you will have increased your available credit (if not maxed out), and you can increase your credit score if you pay your credit card debt on time. However, if you're planning to apply for a mortgage or other major loan in the next year, it's best to avoid churning.

Achieving the minimum spending requirements for the sign-up bonuses for travel credit cards is easily accomplished through using those credit cards for two primary manufactured spending purchases:

1. Buying cash equivalents (e.g., PIN-enabled reload or gift cards) to load onto alternative banking products
2. Directly loading funds onto alternative banking products

Assuming you can use your travel credit card for the purchases, the best places to buy cash equivalents are drugstores, office supply stores, and grocery stores, all of which grant multiple points per dollar spent with certain credit cards, as well as through gift card websites, such as Gift Card Mall. When you buy gift cards online, you must make sure to first go through an online shopping portal, such as eBates, where you can click through to Gift Card Mall in order to earn cash back. Ideally, you want to purchase the maximum gift card denomination (usually $500), because the activation fee can be up to $6.95 per card, regardless of the amount. Thus, buying larger gift cards costs less per transaction than buying smaller gift card denominations. In order to liquidate cash equivalents, you must obtain a physical card, not an electronic card, and the cash equivalents must be PIN enabled. American Express gift cards do not work, while US Bank– and MetaBank-issued cards tend to work the best. It's important to remember that though you are making large purchases, you are not incurring massive amounts of debt, because you will repay these charges each month.

Because there are sometimes issues with liquidating the cash equivalents, it's important to do a test with small amounts of money first. It's also very important to keep receipts and records of your spending transactions. In addition, as previously mentioned, you should always pay your credit card bills within thirty days, because paying credit card fees and interest devalues the miles, points, or savings realized. Since many cash equivalents have activation fees, if you buy these cards using a travel credit card at a retailer—such as a grocery store, where you can earn multiple points per dollar, or via an online shopping portal that provides cash back—you can offset your costs and earn more bang for your buck.

If you use alternative banking products, you must either add funds directly to these banking products via a points-earning credit card or purchase debit and reload cards with a points-earning credit card. Otherwise, this effort is pointless—pun intended. The top three alternative banking products for manufactured spending are listed below:

1. American Express Serve: https://www.serve.com/
2. American Express Bluebird: https://www.bluebird.com/
3. PayPal Business Debit MasterCard: https://www.paypal.com/webapps/mpp/debit-card

The liquidation options for these three alternative banking products may include the following:

- ATM
- Walmart Money Center kiosk or register (Bluebird and Serve only)
- transfer to bank account
- online bill pay
- cash back at grocery store registers
- writing a money order to yourself

Each of these alternative banking products might not allow each of the referenced liquidation options, so familiarize yourself with these products by visiting their official websites. For example, one liquidation option for a prepaid debit gift card is to purchase a money order with the debit gift card, address the money order to yourself, and deposit the money order into your bank account, using the deposited funds to repay the credit card used to purchase the debit gift card. Another method is to use the debit gift card to load one of the alternative banking products, either at a participating retailer or online. These methods work because the debit gift card acts like a bank debit card, but keep in mind that some cash equivalents cannot be purchased with a credit card. Also, it is very important that you do not buy PayPal My Cash Reloads and transfer them from your PayPal account to your bank account, because PayPal will likely shut down your account.

Diversify Your Portfolio

Imagine having 100,000 airline miles—enough for two economy-class airline tickets for a visit to London's Big Ben. Well, if you consider your miles and points a short-term investment, you can achieve an immeasurable return on investment. After becoming familiar with the three major airline alliances and hotel loyalty programs, enroll in airline and hotel programs that you believe you will use, including foreign airline programs, such as Flying Blue (Air France–KLM). Enrolling in the foreign airline programs doesn't mean you actually have to assign the miles you fly to the foreign carrier; it just means you have the ability to transfer points to foreign programs, which sometimes have the best award-redemption prices. For example, Flying Blue, a SkyTeam member, offers award flights from the United States to Europe for 50,000 miles, while Delta (also a SkyTeam member) award flights to Europe cost 60,000. While there is no cost to enrolling in foreign airline programs, many of them pass fuel surcharges in their award flights, which means that a "free" flight in economy class could incur $500 in taxes and fees.

Never travel anywhere without earning miles and points. Of course, having a travel partner doing the same yields twice the results. One key tactic to diversifying your miles and points is tailoring your spending to maximize the points earned for each purchase. For example, if you spend a lot of money on gas and groceries, you will want to choose a travel credit card that offers multiple points per dollar spent in these categories. The same strategy would apply for other bonus spending categories. Other common ways to earn miles and points, as well as cash back, are listed here:

1. <u>Airline and Credit Card Rewards Malls:</u> Most airlines have their own shopping portals (e.g., United, Alaska, JetBlue, American, Delta, American Express, Chase, Citibank), as do the transferable-points programs (e.g., Chase Ultimate Rewards, Citibank, and American Express Membership Rewards).
2. <u>Online survey sites:</u> Take online surveys to earn points or cash via sites such as Opinion Place, Swagbucks, e-Miles, MyPoints, Points for Surveys, Valued Opinions, Miles for Thoughts,

Opinion Miles Club, e-Rewards, etc. The miles earned per transaction will not be large, but every bit counts.

3. Online shopping portals: When buying anything online, always use an online shopping portal. Cashback Monitor provides a comparison of the best rates from sites, such as Coupay, EBates, EVRewards, Big Crumbs, Top Cashback, and Rewards.com, all of which allow you to select retailers through their shopping portals and earn cash back for purchases you were already going to make. The purchases do not have to be travel-related, but sites such as Groupon and LivingSocial—which both offer travel deals—are also options for earning cash back through online shopping portals.

4. Airline Dining Programs: Sign up for airline dining programs, such as MileagePlus Dining and AAdvantage Dining. Once you sign up and register your credit card, you will earn airline miles when you dine at participating restaurants, and many dining programs offer sign-up bonuses.

5. Banking Products: Sometimes banks offer points for obtaining home mortgages or car loans, or for opening checking, savings, and investment accounts (e.g., BankDirect, American HomesMiles, or Wells Fargo Home Mortgage). By banking with BankDirect or obtaining a mortgage via American HomesMiles or Wells Fargo Home Mortgage, you can earn American Airlines Advantage miles. By opening a nonretirement account with Fidelity, you can earn American, Delta, or United miles. These offers are not frequent but can be a great way to earn additional miles.

If keeping a handle on your points seems daunting, sign up for AwardWallet (www.awardwallet.com), because this site is excellent for tracking your points balances. With these portfolio strategies, your points and savings could multiply quickly, becoming your financial bridge to London Bridge.

Using Miles, Points, and Money

Though travel is about having fun, it's also about being smart. That's why you should always seek the best utilization of your money, miles, and points. Airline and hotel loyalty programs are the most effective means to cut travel costs, so figure out which programs you can use for your preferred travel destinations. A general rule of thumb in the travel community is aiming for an award redemption value of 2 cents per point or greater, which means that if a paid fare for a flight costs $1,000 and the award cost is 50,000 airline miles, you would achieve a value of 2 cents per point. The value achieved depends on the cost of paid rates and whether you are using a transferrable or fixed-value program. Taking advantage of airline and hotel loyalty program rules, such as airline stopovers, open-jaw flights, distance-based airline award programs, and hotel best-rate guarantees can make a big difference in maximizing your money, miles, and points.

Utilization Options

When it comes to redemptions, some travel credit cards offer a value of 1 cent for every point redeemed using the fixed-value or pay-with-points concept. This redemption ratio means that a $1,000 flight would cost 100,000 rewards points. However, when it comes to redeeming rewards points for flights, you can get far more value than one cent per point. One way to do so is by using a transferrable-points program to transfer points to airline loyalty programs directly and not by using those points for travel statement credits (i.e., fixed value or paying with points).

Generally, airline miles are better than hotel points because you can receive a greater value for airline miles (e.g., premium cabin flights) than hotel points and have more redemption options, given airline partnerships and rules. So let's say you book an award ticket from the United States to Lisbon that connects in Paris. Depending on the airline's award rules, you can stop over in Paris as well as visit Lisbon for the same number of miles. Now you have seen two places for only the additional cost of award taxes and fees. Premium-class travel represents one of the best uses of airline miles and rewards points. For example, a round-trip business-class flight to Europe can cost $4,000 but averages about 120,000 miles with airline programs. This represents a value of 3 cents per mile or point. For upgrades to premium class on paid tickets using points, you should review an airline's upgrade award chart, contact reservations call centers, and inquire at check-in on the day of travel. It never hurts to know your options, especially when spending fourteen hours flying on a plane.

A few airline programs, such as British Airways, have a distance-based program for redemptions instead of a zone-based program like US-based carriers. One of the best uses of distance-based programs is for short flights. For example, for flights of less than 650 miles in distance, oneworld member British Airways charges as little as 4,000 miles one-way, while American Airlines requires a greater number of miles for the same route. In addition, Star Alliance member Avianca offers competitive redemption rates within its zones, an example being round-trip flights within the northeast United States for 15,000 miles. By contrast, Star Alliance member United charges 25,000 miles round-trip for the same flight. Another perk that is offered by only a few airlines is family pooling of airline miles (e.g., JetBlue, British Airways, and Korean Airlines), and this option offers another great way to maximize airline miles.

Many hotel loyalty programs offer promotions, discounts, rate sales, and free nights via credit cards without using points; and even if using points, many hotel loyalty programs have cash-plus-points options, which allow you to combine a certain number of points with cash for an award night. Hotel credit cards can be very lucrative, as many hotel brands offer free nights for meeting spending requirements with their credit cards and offer multiple points per dollar spent at their hotels. While hotel rates fluctuate, the price to redeem points at hotel stays does not change unless a hotel program changes its tiers or category levels. Thus, you should always check the rates at your hotel to ensure you are getting a great value for using your points.

For other accommodations options, Airbnb offers gift cards that can be purchased with American Express Membership Rewards points, as well as a pay-with-points option, which means that you can obtain free stays at Airbnb properties. And if credit cards are not a payment option, payments can be made via PayPal in most cases, and you can easily fund transactions for PayPal by purchasing PayPal MyCash Reload cards with a rewards credit card, thereby earning points. Another accommodation option, which typically has large units, is timeshare rentals. You don't have to own a timeshare to take advantage of them, as websites like Tug2 and Redweek allow you to rent timeshare units directly from owners, and these costs can usually be paid via PayPal.

To use points for transportation, a fixed-value credit card is the best option, as you can be reimbursed for subway, taxi, rental car, and Uber/Lyft fees. Search rental-car rates on rental-car-company sites, as well as on sites such as Kayak, Hotwire, CarRentals.com, Priceline, and AutoSlash. Hertz's Gold Plus Rewards program offers free standard rentals for 675 points per day and 2,750 points per week—the weekly rental rate being cheaper than the daily rental rate. You can earn Hertz points from car rentals and by buying points, but buying points will not make sense if the cost of the rental is similar to the cost of buying points. You can obtain a $50 Hertz gift certificate for 6,000 Amtrak points, and a $100 Hertz gift certificate for 10,000 Amtrak points.

Remember that you can always be reimbursed via travel statement credits when using fixed-value credit cards to pay for accommodations, flights, fees, and local transportation. And if you have family members who have no interest in earning miles and points, ask if they can use your credit card for payment or put a hotel stay in your name so you can earn additional miles and points.

Booking Awards

Once I pick a destination, I determine whether I want to book an award flight or a paid flight, and I make the same determination for accommodations. If airfares to my preferred destination cost $1,000 or greater, I almost always use rewards points from airlines or travel credit cards because I can extract the most value from my points by doing so. This is especially true during peak travel times, when fares are highest. And since airfare must be paid at the time of booking, I don't have to shell out cash at the onset of booking trips when I use points for flights. If airfares cost less than $300 per person, I usually pay for those flights or get reimbursed for purchasing those flights using rewards points. For less expensive routes, such as those within the United States or to Mexico, paying for the airfare, even if reimbursed with fixed-value credit cards, will allow you to take advantage of discount carriers and earn airline miles for those flights.

If you plan to use miles and points for free flights or hotel stays, book award flights as soon as possible or as soon as seats become available, typically 330 days in advance. You can always cancel award flights for a fee, or for free if you have top-tier elite status. In addition, even after booking award flights, you should continue to check different options, as many seats also become available within two weeks of departure. For free hotel stays, you generally have more flexibility when booking hotel awards, since hotel-room inventory and award availability are usually less of an issue than airline inventory and availability.

To book airline awards online, you should first visit ExpertFlyer or the airline alliance websites referenced in the section "Airline Routes," as these websites will show you the best award-seat inventory for each alliance. To get the best search results, you should perform your flight search as a series of one-way searches and piece together your itinerary with each individual segment. For example, if you want to fly round-trip from New York to Honolulu but you have a connection in San Francisco, you should search for each segment separately. In other words, search for New York to San Francisco and San Francisco to Honolulu. Doing this also allows you to see which individual dates have award seats and which dates don't, which can't be done as easily when searching as a round-trip. From the search results, you want to choose only awards at the Saver level, which represents the lowest level, and not the Standard level, which is usually twice the number of miles as Saver.

Some airline awards can be booked only by calling airline reservations, and there is usually a telephone booking fee of at least $25. When booking airline awards via phone, keep in mind that many reservation specialists do not know their airline's partner airlines or award-routing rules, and it may be necessary to hang up and call again (HUCA) until you get a reservations specialist who is highly knowledgeable of the airline and the airline alliance. If you have a quick issue to resolve with airlines, many of them also offer customer service responses of up to 140 characters via Twitter.

Hotel award bookings are much easier than airline bookings, as inventory is usually much greater and information is more readily available. The best places to score free hotel nights are hotel chains, such as Hilton, Hyatt, and Marriott, so perform award searches by visiting the hotel websites. Take advantage of transferable points, hotel points, hotel promotions, hotel best-rate guarantees, and hotel co-branded credit cards that offer free nights, such as the Hyatt Visa credit card. Some online travel agencies, such as hotels.com, have loyalty programs that offer free nights after meeting certain requirements, and these free nights can be redeemed beyond hotel chain properties. For more information on hotel loyalty programs, see appendix A.

Hotel Best-Rate Guarantees

Another useful trick for lessening the cost of travel is through hotel and online travel agency (OTA) best-rate guarantees. This concept is really no different than price-match guarantees with retail stores, but most hotels and OTAs offer discounts or benefits beyond just matching the price. For hotels, you would book a room on the hotel or OTA website and find the same room at a lower rate on another site. Once you submit your claim, the hotel will drop its price, usually below the competitor's price. The lower price must be publicly available on the competitor's site when the claim is being processed, and you must have found a booking for the same room type with the same rate plan, same dates, same cancellation policy, and for the same number of occupants. You cannot receive a best-rate guarantee based on discounted rates, package deals, discount sites, or auction sites. Some OTA guarantees require competitor websites to be in English and the lower rate to be posted in US dollars, and some have minimum rate requirements, typically $50. Below are some of the noteworthy hotel best-rate guarantees:

Best Western	Will match the competitor's rate and provide $100 Best Western gift card
Choice Hotels	Will match the competitor's rate and provide the first night free
Club Carlson	Will beat the competitor's rate by 25%
Hilton	Will match the competitor's rate and provide a $50 American Express Gift Cheque or a $50 discount.
Hyatt	Will beat the competitor's rate by 20%

IHG	Will match the competitor's rate and provide the first night free
Marriott	Will beat the competitor's rate by 25%
Starwood	Will beat the competitor's rate by 10% or provide 2,000 Starpoints

Below are some of the noteworthy OTA best-rate guarantees:

Expedia	Will refund the difference in price and provide a $50 coupon
Hotels.com	Will refund the difference in price
Orbitz	Will refund the difference in price and provide $50 in Orbucks (higher amounts for Rewards members)
Travelocity	Will refund the difference in price and provide a $50 coupon

Money-Saving Tips

Similar to flight award bookings, to find the lowest airfares for your destination, search early and search often. Even if your trip isn't for a couple of years, you can look now to see what the fare trends are for your preferred destination. And have a few possible dates in mind so you can be flexible about when to go if you find a good deal on certain dates. Google Flight Explorer (www.google.com/flights/explore) shows a calendar of dates by region or by destination up to six months in advance. If you have your eye on a particular destination or deals from your departure city, sign up for fare alerts with the airlines and with travel sites such as ExpertFlyer, Airfarewatchdog, FareCompare, and Google Flights. Hotelwatchdog and Hotel Hustle (offered by Wandering Aramean) are great resources for hotel deal alerts. Other travel sites, such as The Flight Deal, ExitFares, and The Fare Deal Alert provide incredible daily airfare deal alerts, while airline and hotel newsletters, websites, and Twitter handles (e.g., JetBlueCheeps and Alaska Airlines' Fast Dash) are also great ways to learn about travel deals.

When searching airfares, keep in mind that the cheapest days to travel will be those days with the least demand, typically Tuesdays and Wednesdays, while Fridays and Sundays and days around holidays are usually the most high-demand days to travel; and the cheapest times to fly will be early morning and late evenings, including red-eye flights.

Fares are often cheaper when booked forty-five days in advance of travel. If you plan to pay for flights, you should also change your point-of-sale location to find cheaper fares. In other words, whenever you visit a travel booking site, it automatically detects your location, so you will need to change your location to your destination country to possibly find lower rates. The day after booking a flight, you should recheck the price to see if the rate dropped. If the rate dropped, you can cancel an airline itinerary for no charge within twenty-four hours of booking.

Other ways to make travel more affordable are cutting back on expenses and setting up a travel savings account. If you're planning a trip, cut back on nonessential expenses. Perhaps avoid spending money on that daily cup of coffee, spa and beauty treatments, entertainment expenses, or meals at restaurants. I know this might be unpopular, but think of it as temporary. This practice can easily save $200 a month, which can be placed into a travel savings account that is designated specifically to fund your trips. You can also set up direct deposits of your paychecks so that a percentage of your salary is automatically deposited into your travel savings account, with the remainder going to your primary bank account. If you set aside $50 per week, you can save $1,300 per year, which can go a long way toward travel expenses. A great tool for helping you to budget your finances is Mint (www.mint.com), which allows you to track your credit card and bank accounts as well as set a budget.

Anything worth having is worth the time, and while travel hacking takes diligence and effort, it is very useful for building points balances rapidly and lessening the cost of travel. Make sure you're comfortable with pursuing any of the travel-hacking strategies outlined in this book. To further assist you with these concepts, I recommend two noteworthy travel-hacking blogs: *The Points Guy and Million Mile Secrets*. It may seem overwhelming at first, but the benefits are priceless. So if you invest the time and effort into, at least, these five takeaways for step 2, you'll be well on your way to your next vacation:

- Sign up for and familiarize yourself with airline, hotel, and credit card loyalty and rewards programs, and apply for at least one travel credit card that aligns with your spending habits and travel goals.

- Put all spending on travel credit cards while earning the maximum in bonus categories, and pay the entire balances within thirty days.
- Use manufactured spending to meet minimum spending requirements on travel credit cards to earn a substantial amount of miles that would otherwise not be possible
- Aim for a value of at least 2 cents per mile or point when redeeming miles and points for travel.
- Open a separate savings account with your bank and set aside a reasonable amount of money each week to use for future trip costs.

Step 3:

TRAVEL PACKING

Travel packing is an essential part of traveling and an area that can be a real hassle, but it doesn't have to be. Using checklists and adopting efficient methods of packing are important. Don't try to cram a ton of clothes into a weekend bag for a short getaway; and don't pack at the last minute, as you'll be likely to forget essential items if you do. Packing well requires ensuring that you have everything you need for your trip without your baggage being overweight. Doing so guarantees that you can easily access the items in your carry-on baggage that you will need during your flight or for airport screening. By employing a balanced approach, you'll breeze through the check-in and screening processes.

So what essential items should you pack in your suitcase? Below is a checklist of the basic items you should consider taking on your next trip. But before pulling out that suitcase and determining what to pack, always review the TSA security screening procedures (http://www.tsa.gov/travel/security-screening).

What to Pack

Travel Accessories and Toiletries

- ☐ toiletries and toiletry containers
- ☐ toiletry/cosmetics bag, as well as cosmetics
- ☐ sanitizing wipes, hand sanitizer, and facial cleansing wipes in your carry-on

☐ travel-size mouthwash and sugar-free gum
☐ travel pillow

Tech Products and Gadgets

☐ camera
☐ tablet or laptop with case
☐ power cords and chargers for electronic devices (Place all electronics and their power cords or chargers in your carry-on baggage, because you can often charge your device at the airport or on the plane.)
☐ travel adapter, such as the Belkin Global Travel Kit (Most other countries' electrical systems are different from those in the United States, both in the voltage and the design of the outlet plug. Place adapters for charging electronic devices in your carry-on baggage.)
☐ portable speaker

Clothing

☐ a sufficient amount of clothing for one week of travel, tailored to your destination's climate and your planned activities (Try to pack items that can serve multiple purposes [e.g., jeans, yoga pants], and stick to a neutral color palette. Plan to rewear clothes, using a sink to hand wash items or using laundering services.)
☐ Tide Travel Sink Packets and travel laundry hooks (great for allowing you to self-clean your garments in a sink or a portable bag such as the Scrubba Wash Bag; if your accommodation has a washer and dryer, even better)
☐ extra pair of undergarments in your carry-on baggage, to be used in case you are stranded or your luggage is lost
☐ compression socks, which can be worn to the airport
☐ lightweight, insulated, water-resistant jacket or coat
☐ protective clothing and accessories, such as a hat, sunglasses, and UV-rated clothing
☐ walking shoes (can be worn to the airport), flip-flops/sandals, and dress shoes

Food and Health

☐ healthy nonperishable snacks, including nonliquid snacks in your carry-on baggage (Place all snacks in large freezer bags for easy retrieval. You can often buy snacks at the airport, but if you have a favorite snack, you should bring it instead of taking the chance of not finding something you like at the airport or on the flight.)
☐ sufficient prescriptions and other medications or supplements for the duration of your trip (Medications include pain relievers, gas and antidiarrheal pills, sinus allergy medicine, and cold medicine. In many countries you can buy these medications if needed, but it is very convenient to bring the medications you prefer so you don't have to waste time visiting a pharmacy or interpreting the medication's instructions.)
☐ Band-Aids and ointment
☐ sunscreen and insect repellent, if applicable

Miscellaneous

☐ freezer and storage bags, which can keep things clean and easily store loose items.
☐ a dirty clothes bag, which can be a plastic bag or linen bag (You can also use the plastic laundry bag located in the closet of your hotel room.)
☐ painter's tape to place around the lids of toiletries to add another layer of security for preventing the leakage of liquids (Painter's tape is also useful for taping snack bags that you have opened but not finished.)

For more specific packing lists, including by duration and destination, PackPoint (www.packpnt.com) is a very useful app.

How to Pack

Admittedly, packing for a trip is probably my least favorite travel-related activity, although unpacking is a close second. After years of overpacking, disorganization, and trial and error, I finally found a system that works for me. Nowadays, packing requires less thought, which means less stress, so try the following steps when packing your next suitcase.

- Step 1: Lay out all of the clothes and items for your trip.
- Step 2: Pack shoes first. Use a packing shoe bag or a plastic bag to place shoes in the suitcase, orienting each pair facing the opposite direction (heel to toe). Do not pack your shoes uncovered in your suitcase—just think of all the grime and germs on the bottoms of them alone! Pack your socks in your shoes to help them hold their shape and to maximize space. If you have mittens, scarves, or other accessories, place these in the space around the shoe bags.
- Step 3: Organize your clothes by outfit and place them inside packing cubes. To maximize space and prevent creases in your clothes, roll both hard items, such as jeans, and soft items, such as cotton T-shirts. Packing your clothes by outfit and using packing cubes saves time and allows you to avoid sorting through countless clothes items only to find that what you were looking for is actually at the bottom of the suitcase. And you can easily rearrange the packing cubes if you do have to retrieve something. You will also be able to select a cube and essentially have your outfit already planned. You can also place accessories in the packing cube, but avoid packing any expensive items in your checked baggage.
- Step 4: Pack a dirty clothes bag or dirty clothes packing cube on top of your clean clothes packing cubes to store any clothes worn during your trip and to keep them separate from your clean clothes. Insert a dryer sheet in the dirty clothes bag so that when you add the worn clothes, they will be less pungent. I often use hotel laundry bags, which are located in the closet or wardrobe of the hotel room, as my dirty clothes bag. However, my favorite dirty clothes bag is a linen drawstring laundry bag I used and still have from a stay at a Ritz-Carlton property.
- Step 5: On top of the dirty clothes bag, place toiletries, undergarments, belts, collared shirts, and oversize clothing items, such as coats. I use a cosmetics bag to store cosmetics and toiletries, but small packing cubes also work well for cosmetics and toiletries. As an extra precaution, place liquid items in plastic freezer bags and seal the tops with painter's tape to ensure no

leakage. Place extra items, such as undergarments, in either a packing cube or a freezer bag, pressing the air out of the bag to compress it. This ensures that your undergarments are easy to locate and lessens the direct handling of sensitive items by airport security agents. For belts, place them along the inside perimeter of the suitcase. Lastly, place oversize items and collared shirts on top of this layer.

If you plan to take frequent trips and want to try an innovative service, DUFL (www.dufl.com) offers a luxury travel service that will send you a suitcase to load with items you typically wear when traveling. You then ship the case back to DUFL, where the company will store your items. Once you have a trip booked, you use the DUFL app to select the items to pack, and DUFL will ship them in the suitcase to your destination. Once your trip is complete, you arrange at your hotel to send your items back to DUFL for laundering and storage. The cost is $9.95 per month for storage and $99 per round-trip, which includes shipping fees and cleaning services.

Travel Gear

When it comes to traveling, ensuring you have the right travel gear can make all the difference. Choosing travel gear depends on the duration of your trip and your travel style. Before buying new luggage, you should first measure the inside of your existing luggage to see if it meets your needs and to determine what size luggage you have been accustomed to using. If you feel your current luggage is too small, you will need to purchase a larger suitcase. However, keep in mind that the International Air Transport Association (IATA) has recommended that cabin bags be 21.5" × 13.5" × 7.5" to create more storage space on planes. While US-based airlines have not adopted the IATA's recommendations, some international carriers have adopted them. Each carrier sets its own luggage recommendations, and major US carriers have cabin size limits of at least 22" × 14" × 9".

Hard-sided vs. soft-sided is always a hot debate. In general, hard-sided suitcases resist staining and are stronger than soft-sided suitcases, while soft-sided suitcases typically have more compartments and are lighter and more expandable than hard-sided suitcases. My personal preference is for soft-cases, because they are more flexible and lighter, and I usually steer clear of designer luggage, although I do have an affinity for designer totes and handbags.

Over time and through various trips around the world, I have used a variety of luggage, ranging from budget to luxury brands. A few noteworthy brands that I recommend are PacSafe, which sells bags with an antitheft design that deters pickpockets; American Tourister; Traveler's Choice; and Rockland, all of which sell quality budget luggage. For midrange luggage, Samsonite, Travelpro, and Delsey offer wonderful products, while Tumi, Hartmann, and Briggs and Riley are the best examples of function, design, and style. And many high-end luggage brands, such as Briggs and Riley, have lifetime warranties on their products.

I've been able to find great deals on midrange luggage brands, such as Samsonite and Delsey, at TJX stores, Ross Dress for Less, Kohl's, Bed Bath & Beyond, and at department stores during clearance sales. Department stores typically have a greater range than nonluggage retail stores. Online retailers are also great places to find luggage deals, and with most online retailers, such as eBags, you can earn cash back or multiple points per dollar spent when you make purchases through a cash-back site or airline shopping portal. Luggage outlet stores are also great sources, and Samsonite, Hartmann, TravelPro, and Tumi are just a few of the brands with luggage outlets located across the country.

Though packing is a hassle, with the right planning, the hassle factor can be kept to a minimum. Plus, who wouldn't want to have the envious problem of packing for a vacation? That's a problem I didn't mind solving, so now you don't have to. The five takeaways from step 3 are as follows:

- Check TSA's security screening procedures, and be sure that your carry-on luggage will meet the cabin size limitations of the airline. Each airline sets its own limits, and this information can be found on the airline's website.

- Use the basic checklist from the section "What to Pack" to be sure you've packed the essential travel items. Use a travel app, such as PackPoint, for a more comprehensive checklist.
- Follow the five recommended packing steps from the "How to Pack" section to organize items in your suitcase effortlessly.
- Evaluate the size, style, and durability of your existing luggage to make sure it fits your needs.
- If you're in the market for new luggage, you can find deals at outlet stores, discount retailers, department stores, and online.

Step 4:

TRAVEL INSURANCE

Let's face it—you don't need insurance until you need insurance, and travel insurance is no different. Whether you're skiing in the Alps or just walking down the *avenida*, the unexpected can always occur. That's why you need to be knowledgeable of the different types of travel insurance—so you can be justly compensated or reimbursed if you have delays or missing baggage or need to cancel altogether. In general, travel insurance can be grouped into seven types: trip protection, baggage protection, rental-car coverage, travel accident insurance, travel and emergency assistance, travel health insurance, and evacuation insurance. Trip protection, baggage protection, and rental-car coverage are the most common types of travel-insurance options being covered by travel credit cards, such as American Express and Citi. However, most credit card benefits have a lot of fine print and are not adequate for major areas, such as medical and evacuation insurance.

I typically travel only with items I could live without, so I don't devote much thought to baggage-protection insurance, since losing those items would not be a great financial loss. This is not to say that you shouldn't be knowledgeable of and claim any insurance benefits you have. However, I often book award flights, and baggage-protection benefits are usually not covered by travel credit cards, because the entire cost of the airfare must be booked on a travel credit card in order to claim benefits—and award flights have only the cost of taxes and fees. In addition, sometimes only the cardholder is covered by a travel credit card's insurance benefits, so this is an area where buying additional travel insurance can make sense. For tech items and other expensive items, be sure to document their make and model and photograph them, so that if they are lost, stolen, or damaged through no fault of your own, you will have sufficient documentation of them. As for travel accident insurance, such as accidental death and dismemberment, you will already be covered if you have term life insurance, so it's worth considering only if you don't have other insurance that covers you.

The most important types of travel insurance are travel health insurance and evacuation insurance. Think of travel health insurance as emergency health insurance, not for preventive or routine care; and evacuation insurance is as the name implies. If you have domestic medical coverage, you need to know if you are covered overseas and what you are covered for specifically. If you do not have medical insurance in the United States, it is wise to consider purchasing travel health insurance. If you have a preexisting condition, you need a plan that explicitly covers the condition. The insurance type that is not usually covered through any other means is evacuation insurance. If there were a medical emergency, wouldn't you be glad to know that you could be repatriated back home?

Travel-insurance premiums are dependent on the total trip cost, coverage type, and the age of the traveler. You can expect to pay up to 10 percent of the total trip cost for travel insurance. Regardless of the coverage you elect, you need to fully understand what your plan covers and, if you have evacuation insurance, that it covers repatriation to your home airport by air ambulance. The following section provides an overview of the seven types of travel insurance.

Types of Travel Insurance

Trip Protection

- trip cancellation—This is coverage for a trip that must be cancelled before departure for a covered reason, which typically excludes airline cancellations or flight changes.
- trip interruption—This coverage reimburses prepaid nonrefundable trip costs in the event that a trip is interrupted for a covered reason.

- trip delays—This coverage provides reimbursement, typically for meals and accommodations, in the event of covered departure or return delays. Trip delays can become trip cancellations.
- missed connection—This benefit reimburses a specific amount per day for expenses if the cause is related to the carrier or weather.

Unlike in Europe, there is no federal requirement for US-based airlines to provide benefits to passengers in the event of flight delays. In general, if the delay is flight-wide, such as a delay due to weather or a mechanical issue, the airlines will not compensate you. However, the airlines should offer placement on another flight without any fees, and if your flight is cancelled or extremely delayed, you are entitled to cancel your flight and receive a refund of the unused portion of your costs. Sometimes the airline will provide accommodation if you must stay overnight, but this does not usually happen if the airline claims no fault. If you are involuntarily bumped from a flight (which means it's not a flight-wide issue), you are entitled to compensation if the airline cannot get you to your destination near the same time as your original flight. Airlines also offer compensation when you voluntarily give up your seats on an overbooked flight. For more information, check out the airline's contract of carriage. Many travel credit cards provide some trip protection coverage, usually for nonrefundable costs and for covered reasons only. In addition, the coverage usually has an annual cap. Chase travel credit cards tend to have the most generous reimbursement limits.

Baggage Protection

- lost baggage—Baggage coverage provides replacement value for lost, stolen, or damaged baggage as well as the contents of the baggage. One thing to consider is single-item limits, which are often restricted to $500. Therefore, separate coverage may be needed.
- delayed baggage—Coverage for delayed baggage provides a certain amount to cover essential items, such as toiletries and clothing.

Some credit cards offer baggage-protection coverage that is comparable to purchased travel-insurance plans. For example, with the Citi Thank You Preferred credit card, you are covered up to $3,000 per person, per trip ($2,000 per person, per bag, per trip for New York residents) if items are lost, stolen, or damaged by an airline for a trip purchased with your Citi credit card. However, you must pay for your entire ticket with your credit card, which means that award tickets, for which you only pay the applicable taxes and fees, are not covered. Be sure to keep the checked luggage tracking tags that the airline representative affixes to your boarding pass at the check-in desk in order to be reimbursed.

Rental-Car Coverage

This benefit covers the cost of repairs and rental charges imposed by the rental company. Some credit cards provide collision damage waiver (CDW) and car-rental-loss insurance benefits, which exclude liability coverage but generally cover theft or damage when you pay with your credit card and decline the rental company's insurance. Rental-car insurance via credit cards is usually secondary to your primary car insurance. However, the Chase Sapphire Preferred card offers primary rental-car insurance, which means you don't have to submit a claim to your auto insurer. In addition, American Express offers a primary car insurance option for a fee through its Premium Car Rental Protection program. Be advised that some credit cards exclude some countries, so be sure to read the policy prior to booking. Chase also offers CDW insurance as primary insurance with the Chase Sapphire Preferred card, reimbursing you up to the actual cash value of the vehicle.

Travel Accident Insurance

- accidental death and dismemberment (AD&D)—Accidental death and dismemberment coverage pays an indemnity up to the covered amount for the loss of life or functioning limbs to you or your beneficiary.
- flight accident—Flight accidents are those that occur during the airline portion of a trip, and it might be included in some travel-insurance plans as AD&D.

Because of the rarity of airplane accidents, flight accident insurance is not worth purchasing as supplemental coverage. However, if it is already being included as a part of a travel-insurance package, no problem.

Travel and Emergency Insurance

- emergency assistance / concierge services—This benefit provides assistance with arranging medical services or other emergency consultations. It does not provide any evacuation or medical services, only assistance with finding such services.

This insurance type is a common added benefit of most rewards credit cards and purchased travel insurance, so there is no need to specifically request it. If you need assistance before or during a trip, services are available 24-7 for emergency travel arrangements, travel issues, medical and legal referrals, and much more. You won't have to scramble to find services close to your location or worry about asking for help when you don't speak the language.

Travel Health Insurance

Some health insurance carriers in the United States provide coverage for emergencies that occur while traveling abroad. However, in many instances, during an emergency abroad, you will have to pay expensive medical bills directly and be reimbursed by your primary health insurance. If your health plan does not cover medical expenses abroad, you can opt to purchase coverage in case of emergencies, and in many instances, the travel medical insurance will pay the costs directly. The cost of this type of insurance increases with age. Be sure to inquire about travel medical insurance for preexisting conditions, if applicable.

Evacuation Insurance

- medical evacuation insurance—Provides coverage for such benefits as emergency medical evacuation, repatriation, reunion, and emergency assistance services. This benefit can also provide payment for travel expenses for one person to be reunited with the hospitalized traveler.
- security, natural disaster, and political evacuation insurance— This coverage pays for the costs to exit a country because of unsafe conditions, such as political events, uprisings, attacks, and natural disasters. This type of insurance should be purchased

immediately after booking your trip, because if an event occurs in the country prior to your trip, you may not be able to add this insurance. And in the case of security or terrorism coverage, most policies cover only those incidents that are deemed terrorism by the US Department of State.

The Citi Prestige card, which has a $450 annual fee and a $250 airline credit, offers up to $100,000 in medical evacuation costs if your entire trip is booked using the card, and the card also has trip protection, baggage protection, rental-car coverage, and travel accident coverage.

Buying Travel Insurance

When it comes to vacation, you probably don't want to think about travel insurance and something going wrong and would much prefer to think about rest and relaxation. But planning for a potential emergency before a trip is much easier than dealing with one during a trip. In addition, you should also understand the lost baggage, trip cancellation, and trip delay benefits provided by your credit card, if applicable. In some cases, you can purchase cancel-for-any-reason coverage, which allows you to cancel for any reason. This coverage, which reimburses a percentage of your prepaid, nonrefundable costs, is usually an add-on to a comprehensive package, and you usually must purchase it within thirty days of your initial trip payment. To ensure that you are adequately insured for travel, consider purchasing the following coverage:

- additional baggage coverage for expensive single items, if the value of your baggage is not covered by credit card benefits
- trip cancellation insurance up to the cost of your trip, if not covered by credit card benefits
- at least $1 million in travel medical insurance
- at least $1 million in personal liability coverage for claims that may be made against you
- medical evacuation and repatriation in case you cannot travel home on a commercial flight
- coverage for any preexisting medical conditions

The various types of travel insurance are usually sold in comprehensive packages. If you're planning to take several trips in a given year or are a frequent traveler, annual or multitrip insurance might make sense and save cents for you. TravelGuard (www.travelguard.com) offer these types of multitrip plans.

You should always compare prices as well as terms and conditions on travel-insurance policies, and never assume that the insurance packages offered by travel agents or as add-ons via airline and travel websites are the best options. Three of the best comparison travel-insurance websites are InsureMyTrip (www.insuremytrip.com), which was the first online travel-insurance rate comparison site; SquareMouth (www.squaremouth.com), which offers a Zero Complaint Guarantee; and World Nomads (www.worldnomads.com), which is a great resource for backpackers and long-term travelers. Unlike some medical evacuation insurance coverage, which will transport you only to the nearest hospital, MedjetAssist (www.medjetassist.com) will transport you to the United States as part of your membership.

While evacuation insurance and travel health insurance are the two most important types of travel insurance, the hope is that you never have to use them. Still, it's great to have peace of mind knowing you are covered if something goes wrong. At a minimum, you should have handy a number to call for travel and emergency assistance, a benefit that is offered through most credit cards and travel-insurance policies. The five takeaways of step 4 are as follows:

- Familiarize yourself with the seven major types of travel insurance.
- Pay for trips entirely with a travel credit card and be informed about the travel-insurance coverage offered.
- Supplement credit card travel-insurance coverage with coverage purchased from travel-insurance companies, when necessary. Read the fine print for all travel insurance.
- Compare rates using the recommended travel-insurance companies.
- Never assume that travel agents offer the best travel-insurance rates.

Step 5:

TRAVEL TIPS

Now that you have picked a destination, adopted a few travel hacks, learned to pack better, and compared travel-insurance options, let's look at how to make the actual experience of traveling better. Step 5 helps you make the most of experiencing your destination by providing advice on travel preparation, technology and apps, healthy habits, tipping, and cultural immersion.

Trip Preparation

Travel is the fun part; travel preparation—not so much. However, these twenty travel-preparation steps will ensure that you have taken the necessary actions prior to travel.

1. Check your vaccination record, and obtain any required or strongly recommended vaccinations. Check the Centers for Disease Control's website for vaccination information.
2. Check to see if you need a visa at the State Department (www.travel.state.gov) for US citizens or at Visa HQ (www.visahq.com/).
3. Ensure that your passport does not expire within six months of your trip. Some countries will not allow you to enter the country if your passport expires within six months.
4. Ensure that the name on your reservation matches that on your passport.

5. Inform your credit card companies of your travel plans so your overseas expenditures are not flagged as suspicious. To make the process smoother, ensure that you have telephone PIN numbers for debit and credit cards as well as the collect-call numbers for the banks.

6. Find out how much it will cost to use your US mobile phone for data and voice at your planned destination or whether your mobile phone provider has international data plans. Make sure that you have an activated international SIM card or an "unlocked" phone.

7. Use the travel checklist found in step 3 to ensure that you have packed the basic travel necessities.

8. Take pictures of valuable items—such as tablets, jewelry, etc.— that you will be bringing on the trip, including serial and model numbers. Use your cell phone and a cloud-based service to store the pictures so they can be accessed anywhere.

9. A few days before departure, hydrate by drinking lots of water and get plenty of sleep. Doing so will help your immune system and combat jet lag.

10. At your residence, arrange to have mail delivery suspended if you will be traveling for more than a week.

11. If checking baggage, place a colorful luggage tag on your checked baggage for easier retrieval at the baggage-claim area.

12. Prior to departure, download apps that you might use. Suggestions for apps can be found in the subsection "Useful Travel Apps and Services."

13. Check-in online and print your boarding passes, if you're not checking bags or if you are flying on a discount/low-cost airline carrier. Though it may not save time, printing boarding passes is a good idea because it's usually better to have printed documents.

14. In addition to boarding passes, print all reservation e-mails for hotels, flights, rental cars, and tours. While having this information stored on a mobile device is very convenient, it is much easier to access and provide printed documents to check-in agents than provide information on a mobile phone. In addition, if documents are not downloaded to your device, accessing them from a mobile phone may be difficult, given unpredictable Internet access.

15. Make sure to charge all of your electronic devices before you travel. Not only will this give your device longer life, but it may also be necessary to avoid having your item confiscated. For example, in India, passengers must power up all electronic devices in order to pass with them through airport security.
16. Check Internet news sites for any events, such as elections, in the countries you will be traveling to. This will ensure awareness of national events that may be occurring. Also, check the US State Department website for basic travel information and travel advisories.
17. Bring enough cash for short-term needs, but use a no-fee debit card at ATMs for the best exchange rates. Of course, your first option should be using a travel credit card with no foreign transaction fees.
18. Double check to make sure you know where your passport is and where you will store it during your flight or flights. Bring a photocopy of your passport.
19. Always check flight status before leaving home.
20. If you drive to the airport, use your smartphone to take a picture of the parking row marker or nearest airport parking lot bus stop so you can remember where you parked upon return. There's nothing worse than carrying luggage around an airport parking lot or garage after a long flight because you forgot where you parked.

At the Airport

Arriving at the airport on time is secretly one of the most exciting parts of your trip because it marks the beginning of your vacation. And with the perks offered by trusted traveler programs and airport lounges, navigating the airport can actually be a fluid, if not enjoyable, experience.

Trusted Traveler Programs

To make your departure and reentry smoother on international flights, I strongly recommend enrolling in a trusted traveler program, such as Global Entry. Global Entry costs $100 for a five-year period and provides expedited reentry into the United States from international travel for US citizens and permanent residents. Citizens of the Netherlands, South Korea, Panama, Canada, Germany, and Mexico are also eligible to participate in Global Entry via their own programs. Global Entry abroad is being expanded to several countries. I got a chance to take advantage of using Global Entry abroad for a flight from Dublin, Ireland, to Washington, DC, where I avoided an hour-long wait in the US preclearance section of the Dublin airport. Since I had already undergone customs procedures in Dublin, I did not need to deal with any formalities when I landed in Washington, DC.

When enrolling in Global Entry as a US citizen, you will have to be interviewed in person by a US Customs and Border Protection (CBP) official at the nearest enrollment center. Your fingerprints will be taken, and you will undergo a thorough background check in multiple federal government databases. However, once you're approved, you'll be able to submit your customs declaration form at a Global Entry kiosk at the airport instead of completing the paper form given by flight attendants on the plane. Global Entry can save lots of time and is well worth the twenty-dollar annual cost. If traveling with another person, that person also has to have Global Entry in order to receive expedited reentry. You will still be subject to random searches and screening of your bag. Before enrolling, make sure that Global Entry is available at your home airport, as not all airports offer the program.

One of the added perks of the Global Entry program is that it also offers you access to TSA's Pre-Check program, which allows trusted US travelers to bypass traditional TSA security checkpoints and procedures, thereby receiving expedited screening. My first experience with TSA Pre-Check was actually during a pilot phase of the program, as I was not a member of a trusted traveler program. I did not have to take off my shoes or remove liquids or electronic devices, and I went through security in record time! I loved it. You just have to ensure that you enter your trusted traveler number when you make your flight booking. If you have elite status with an airline or are flying in premium class, there are priority screening lines you can use, but these are different from TSA Pre-Check.

Another useful trusted traveler program offered to United States and Canadian citizens is Mobile Passport Control, a free service officially launched by CBP in 2014. By downloading the Mobile Passport Control app, users can submit their flight information, customs declarations information, and a photo to expedite reentry into the United States.

Airport Screening

When navigating through airport screening, I always remove items from my pockets and place my watch in my purse until I get through screening. I don't usually wear belts, but if you can wear one that is free of metal, you will be better off. I usually wear a jacket to the airport and use it to line the screening bins so that I can place liquids, tablets, and other items in the bins without having them come into contact with dirty screening bins. The jacket can easily be washed later. I also wear shoes that are easy to remove and put back on.

Once through airport screening, I always check the monitors to reconfirm gate information and walk to the gate as soon as possible to reconfirm the departure gate in person. If overseas, this is really important, as people line up at the gate as soon as it is announced. If flying on budget carriers overseas, it may be worthwhile to purchase priority boarding. I found this service useful on Ryanair. However, sometimes you don't board the plane from a sky bridge but have to be transported via a bus, and sometimes you will not get priority boarding on the plane because of this. TripAdvisor's Gate Guru (www.gateguru.com) and FlightAware (www.flightaware.com) are great resources for navigating airports, as they track gate information and itineraries as well as provide information on nearby amenities in the airport. In addition, some airports have their own apps, which might be worth downloading if you have to spend considerable time on a layover.

Airport Lounges

Once you have passed through airport security, a lot of times you're stuck waiting at the airport gates, and some do not provide comfortable seating if you can get seating at all. That's why you might want to consider obtaining access to airport lounges, especially if your layover is long. Some perks of airport lounges are free Wi-Fi; complimentary snacks, drinks, newspapers, and magazines; usually cleaner and quieter facilities; and, sometimes, showers. Before purchasing lounge access, peruse loungeguide.net (www.loungeguide.net), SkyTrax (www.airlinequality.com), Wandering Aramean (www.wandr.me), or LoungeBuddy (www.loungebuddy.com), which are sites offering reviews of airline lounges. LoungeBuddy even allows you to purchase lounge access at the airport with its app. There a few ways to obtain access to airport lounges:

1. Purchase a day pass. United, Delta, and American offer day passes to their airport lounges for $50 per person, and you don't have to fly on their flights in order to access the lounges. However, US airline lounge passes tend to be for domestic lounges, not international lounges.
2. Purchase an annual airline membership. These can cost up to $450, but be sure that a participating lounge is located at your home airport before buying. You might also be able to pay for membership with frequent flyer miles.
3. Purchase access via a third-party company. This route is usually most beneficial for international travelers who do not have elite status with an airline. Priority Pass is one of the most popular vendors, and it has more than 700 lounges worldwide. The company offers three packages: Standard, which comes with a $99 annual fee and a $27 fee per visit; Standard Plus, which comes with ten visits for a $249 annual fee; and Prestige, which comes with unlimited airport lounge access for $399 per year. For each plan, guests of the member must pay $27 per visit. Diners Club also offers airport lounge access at more than 500 airport lounges for about $30 per visit; Lounge Pass offers access to 250 lounges worldwide for as low as £13.50; and Lounge Club offers more than 350 airport lounges worldwide.
4. Obtain a credit card that offers airport lounge access. The American Express Platinum card offers access to Delta Sky Clubs, Airspace Lounges, and Centurion Lounges, as well as providing Priority Pass Select membership (requiring cardmembers to enroll in the program). The card comes with a $450 annual fee, but there are other benefits to owning the card,

such as a $200 airline credit, so the airport lounge access is an added benefit. Other credit cards offering lounge access are the Delta Reserve credit card, which provides access to Delta Sky Clubs; the Ritz Carlton Rewards credit card, which offers access to Lounge Club; United MileagePlus credit cards, which offer access to United and Star Alliance lounges worldwide; and the Citi Prestige credit card, which provides Admirals Club access when flying on American Airlines as well as Priority Pass Select membership. All of these credit cards have sizable annual fees but also provide benefits beyond airport lounge access.

5. Obtain airline elite status or fly on a premium-class ticket. Typically you will get free access to airport lounges only if you have midtier elite status, such as Star Alliance Gold status, or if you are flying in premium class.

Flying Tips

Just because you have to get on a plane doesn't mean you have to suffer. One key step to feeling your best is to get rest prior to your trip. The last thing you should do before a flight is stay up late or party until dawn, because doing so will greatly increase your chances of getting sick abroad. If you will be landing at your destination during the early morning, be sure to sleep on the plane so you get some rest and can hit the ground running. If you will be landing at night, try to stay awake during most of the flight so you will be sleepy when you arrive at your destination. For more specificity, Jet Lag Rooster (www.jetlagrooster.com) will incorporate your flight details to create a jet lag plan.

You should also stay hydrated and mobile during the flight by drinking plenty of fluids (avoid caffeine and alcohol) and stretching your legs periodically. And don't rely on the airline to provide snacks, as you might get hungry or not like your options. Bringing your own tasty treats will ensure a more comfortable flight. For soothing sleep, download a white noise app, and don't forget the travel-size hand sanitizer, sanitizing wipes, lip balm, and hand lotion. Though expensive, Hibistat wipes kill bacteria and viruses for up to six hours and are great for the plane. To make your flight as comfortable as possible, be sure to pack useful conveniences, such as compression socks, an eye mask, a travel pillow, noise-cancelling headphones, disposable toothbrushes, sugarless gum, and an infinity scarf.

Take advantage of technology during the flight. If the airplane has an entertainment system, by all means, use it to play games, listen to music, or watch movies. Watching movies is a great way to pass the numerous hours spent flying. You can also use your own devices for these activities, as well as read a book, either printed or digital. For in-flight Internet access, you can opt to buy wireless Internet via services such as Gogo Inflight, which has options ranging from a one-hour pass to unlimited Gogo Wi-Fi. The American Express Platinum Business card provides cardholders ten complimentary Gogo Inflight Wi-Fi passes and also offers complimentary unlimited access to Boingo Wireless Wi-Fi hotspots worldwide. For added wireless Internet security, try PrivateWiFi (www.privatewifi.com). Other technology options are Jott (www.jott.com) and FireChat (www.opengarden.com/firechat), two mesh networking apps that work independently of Wi-Fi and cellular service and that use Bluetooth technology to enable a user to send text messages to another user who has the app.

Staying Connected

Even though the real point of most vacations is to unplug and relax, it's still nice to stay connected to friends and family back home. Most major US cellular providers offer international plans, but you can end up paying dearly if you don't understand the rates and coverage, which is why I have provided three options for staying connected abroad, including summarizing the international data plans for the four major US cellular providers under option A.

Option A: Use your Existing Plan

AT&T—AT&T Passport

- unlimited text messaging and Wi-Fi in more than eighteen countries
- Passport: $30 for 120 megabytes of data; overage of 25 cents per megabyte; calls are $1 per minute

- Passport Plus: $60 for 300 megabytes of data; overage of 20 cents per megabyte; calls are $.50 per minute
- Passport Pro: $120 for 800 megabytes of data; overage of 15 cents per megabyte; calls are $.035 per minute

Sprint—International Plans

Sprint has an International Value Roaming Plan, which offers unlimited data and text to more than twenty countries, mostly in Latin America and Western Europe, with calls for $.20 per minute. The data speeds are only up to 2G, but the service is free, so you just need to activate it online or by calling Sprint. Sprint also offers the following international data pack add-ons:

Canada/Mexico Data Roaming

- $30 for 55 megabytes
- $75 for 175 megabytes
- $125 for 325 megabytes
- overage of $4 per megabyte for each plan

Multiple-Country Data Roaming

- $40 for 40 megabytes
- $80 for 85 megabytes
- overage of $10 per megabyte for each plan

T-Mobile—Simple Choice Plan

T-Mobile's Simple Choice Plan includes data roaming comprising unlimited talk, text, and data in 120 countries for only $50 a month with no yearly contract.

- free unlimited international data in more than 140 countries
- calling and texting in Canada and Mexico the same as in the United States

- $50 for unlimited, talk, text, and data in more than 120 countries with $30 additional for a second line
- $10 for 3 gigabytes additional; $20 for 5 gigabytes additional; and $30 for unlimited gigabytes under the Simple Choice Plan

Verizon—International Plans

TravelPass

- deducts minutes, text, and data from your existing domestic plan while overseas
- $2 per day for Canada and Mexico; $10 per day in more than 65 countries
- the daily fee is incurred only on the days you use it in the eligible country

Global Roaming

- global plan: $25 per 100 megabytes in more than 140 countries; for $15 per month additional, add 100 minutes, 100 text messages, and unlimited received text messages (If you go over, there are no overage charges and you will be billed another $25 for 100 megabytes.)
- pay-as-you-go rates:
    - o global voice starts at $0.89 per minute
    - o global messaging (SMS) is $0.50 per message sent and $0.05 per message received
    - o global data is $2.05 per megabyte in Canada, $5.12 per megabyte in Mexico, and $20.48 per megabyte for the rest of the world
- cruise ship rates: $2.49 per minute for voice roaming, $0.50 per message sent and $0.05 per message received, and $20.48 per megabyte

Option B: Use an International SIM Card

In the United States, mobile phones use either CDMA (Verizon and Sprint) or GSM (T-Mobile and AT&T) technologies, while the rest of the world mostly uses GSM. Therefore, to use an international SIM card, an unlocked GSM-supported phone is required. AT&T will allow you to unlock your phone up to five times for international travel if you are still under contract, and permanently if your contract has expired. Once your phone is unlocked, you would purchase a SIM card abroad for use on a local network, such as Vodafone or Orange. Usually this practice requires spending time in a local mobile phone retailer and purchasing a prepaid plan. Calls to your phone would result in those calling you paying international rates. Another option is data-only SIM card plans, such as One SimCard and MTX Connect.

Additionally, you can use the Google Voice app to receive unlimited text messages and voice mail. To use the Google Voice app on your phone overseas, you will need to make sure to set your preferences to e-mail notifications for missed calls. You will not be receiving calls directly, but you can use a Wi-Fi connection to check your voice mail as well as call a US number by clicking the phone icon within Google Chat.

Option C: Use Wi-Fi and Apps

The most affordable option for staying connected abroad appears to be using free Wi-Fi along with apps. In order to not be charged, make sure to turn off international data on your phone. Most hotels, cafés, and airports offer free Wi-Fi, but heavy data users might also benefit from setting up a personal hotspot, such as Boingo, which costs $7.95 for international Wi-Fi on up to four mobile devices. For owners of Nexus phones, Google Project Fi offers unlimited domestic talk and text, unlimited international text, Wi-Fi tethering, and mobile access in more than 120 countries for the same rate as in the United States.

One cool thing about apps is that you can do text messaging and video chatting through popular products such as WhatsApp, Google Hangouts, FaceTime, Viber, and Skype. And with Skype, you can use the call-forwarding feature to forward incoming Skype calls to another Skype contact for free. To forward incoming Skype calls to a mobile number or landline, you will need to purchase Skype credits (which are like prepaid minutes) or a Skype number, which requires a subscription. If you want to use Skype credits, your forwarded calls will be charged at Skype's pay-per-minute rates. Using Italy as an example, calls via Skype using credits would cost no more than $0.10 per minute, and text messages would cost $0.127 per text message, as opposed to $0.50 per text message for some cellular carriers.

Another cost-effective avenue to stay in touch with others is social media. However, be very careful about broadcasting your real-time travel plans, as doing so can make you a target for criminal activity back home. My advice is to share details and photos from your trip when you return home.

Health and Hygiene

Something I have found in most countries I have visited is an emphasis on and pride in eating freshly prepared meals. "You are what you eat," is a popular phrase that I have heard throughout life. If you eat a lot of processed and artificial foods that your body was not designed to consume, you will feel lethargic, since these foreign substances contribute to inflammation in the body. Unfortunately, airports and airplanes do not provide many healthy food options and are not the cleanest places on earth, which puts you at a greater risk of getting sick at the onset of your vacation. That's why it's vital that you wash your hands frequently. Neglecting to wash one's hands is the number-one way to get sick anywhere (at home or abroad). So keep your hands clean and avoid touching your face. I highly recommend using hand sanitizers often.

Getting sick abroad is one of the worst experiences ever! Mummy tummy, Delhi belly, and Montezuma's revenge are just a few slang terms for getting food poisoning abroad. It happened to me so frequently that I had to change my eating habits when abroad. As a result, within North America, the Caribbean, and Europe, I eat meals the same way as in the United States, but outside these regions, I take a different approach. If you have a sensitive stomach like me, you can take the following precautions when eating abroad, at least at the beginning of your vacation. And if you have food allergies or intolerances, or drug allergies, SelectWisely (www.selectwisely.com) and Triumph

Dining (www.triumphdining.com) provide cards translated into several languages that you can carry with you to present at restaurants.

- Eat only cooked food, which means no salads, thin-skinned or sliced fruits, cold vegetables, sushi, and cold-cut deli meats.
- Avoid dairy and fish.
- Wash your hands frequently.
- Avoid street food unless it is freshly prepared and visibly clean. Sometimes street food is prepared in untreated water, which can cause upset stomach and illness.
- Drink only bottled water, not tap water. Sparkling water helps with digestion. Coffee and tea are generally safe.

While the above list may seem very restrictive, getting sick is far worse than avoiding certain foods. You can also take the hybrid approach and avoid some of these foods to see how you feel, because after all, eating right does not mean sacrificing enjoying local foods, as trying new things is one of the highlights of travel. Just make sure you're careful about where you eat and that you eat a balanced diet, because eating lots of sugary carbohydrates will deplete energy levels. Taking supplemental vitamins can boost your nutrient levels during your trip.

As mentioned in step 3, the following medications should be taken with you: pain relievers, gas and antidiarrheal pills, cold medicine, and sinus allergy medicine. Of course, if you go to Europe, there are plenty of pharmacies that can help you find these items, although maybe more expensively. If you are in need of medical assistance and don't have access to emergency assistance services via travel insurance or credit card benefits, mPassport (www.mpassport.com) offers a paid service that will help you find English-speaking doctors worldwide.

Exploring the Destination

Money and Currency Exchange

Using credit cards without foreign transaction fees while overseas should be your first priority, because you will get the best exchange rate with no fees and the added benefit of rewards points. However, in many countries, even if a vendor accepts credit cards, that vendor might pass along credit card fees to use a credit card, and they might not take American Express, which is less widely accepted than Visa or MasterCard. In addition, in many places, such as street markets and local shops, paying in cash is still the lay of the land. If paying in cash, always pay in the local currency and not in US dollars to avoid being subject to the conversion rates a local vendor requests. To find out the daily exchange rates, use currency conversion tools such as Oanda (www.oanda.com) and XE Currency (www.xe.com), as these sites have apps that are great to download and use for checking rates while exploring your destination. If you need cash, it is best to load up on cash from an ATM at the airport, provided your home bank does not charge outrageous fees. To avoid ATM fees altogether, consider obtaining a debit card from a Schwab Bank High Yield Investor checking account, which doesn't charge ATM fees. If you must exchange cash at a currency exchange carrying booth, currency exchange places in the nontouristy parts of town will give you better rates. Never use a debit card overseas. In fact, never use a debit card anywhere if you don't have to, as you will be putting your finances at risk of theft. Using credit cards is the safer option.

Tipping Etiquette

To tip or not to tip? That is a really good question! Do you need to shell out 20 percent or 20 cents? Tipping varies widely by country and region of the world, and cash tips are always preferred over credit card tips because the recipient gets the money directly. In Egypt and India, tipping is very much accepted, while within Southeast Asian countries, from Thailand to the Philippines, restaurant gratuities are usually already included, so tipping is generally not expected. Tipping in China, South Korea, and Japan is not expected, but in the Caribbean and North America, gratuity isn't usually included, so tipping is the norm. In South America, gratuity is often included in restaurants, but it is acceptable to tip for other services, except in Peru. In Europe, tipping varies widely, although in Iceland and Scandinavia tips are not expected. In the Middle East, gratuity is usually included in restaurant bills, with higher tips expected in the wealthier countries, such as Bahrain, Qatar, and the United Arab Emirates. Tipping is not customary in Australia,

New Zealand, or Oceania, but it's okay if you have been provided exceptional service. Be sure to check your bill to see if a gratuity is being added before tipping, and when in doubt, leave a little extra. For tipping advice on your mobile device, download the Global Tipping app, GlobeTipping, or Tip Calculator Free, as these apps provide country-specific guidance for numerous countries around the world.

Local Transportation Options

Airport Transit: I always have a plan for getting from the airport to my accommodations, and I usually prebook transportation, because the last thing I want to do is figure out how to get somewhere after a long flight with bags in tow. In order to find the best means to traveling to your accommodations, check your hotel's website first, if staying in a hotel. Although the cost of booking transportation through your hotel may be more expensive, it's a good idea to ask the hotel's rates. Bookings via the hotel are very convenient, and you can usually charge the transportation cost to your room bill. You should also check your destination airport's website for official airport transportation options, which include airport shuttles or buses, taxis, and public and private transportation. Other airport transportation options are airport taxis, Uber, Lyft, and GroundLink, a chauffeured black car service operating in more than 100 countries. For a reference guide to taxi costs worldwide, check out TaxiFareFinder (www.taxifarefinder.com).

Rail: Traveling via train is usually more efficient and a lot less time-consuming than air travel, as you can often connect with the subway and arrive and depart from the center of the city. One of the most economical means to travel around Europe is via the Eurail pass, which is offered to non-European citizens of select countries and must be purchased before arrival in Europe. The pass allows you to buy a specific number of days of rail travel during a specific period of time within one country, one region, or multiple countries. The pass is good for specific trains that require no reservation; you just have to ensure you are riding on a covered train. Several years ago, I was traveling from Barcelona to Nice and had booked and confirmed my reservation with a representative in person, only to find out that the train I boarded was not covered, so I was nearly thrown off a train at 2:00 a.m. at an outdoor train stop in the middle of Nowhere, Spain. The train operators did not take credit cards, but they accepted dollars, and luckily, I had enough dollars to pay the fare. So, in summary, if you plan to do a lot of country hopping by train, the pass would be a good option. However, if you are not sure that you will be traveling much by train and want to be flexible and more spontaneous in your travel plans, you can easily purchase individual tickets at the station. You can buy European rail tickets through a US-based site, such as Rail Europe (where you can purchase a pass); on the website of a European national railway, such as SNCF; or directly at the train station. For comprehensive transit service information in Europe, DB Navigator is the best application because it offers real-time data for regional and intracountry trains, subways, buses, and trams. Outside of Europe, Rome2Rio (www.rome2rio.com) and Seat 61 (www.seat61.com) are two of the best sites for searching how to get from point A to point B.

Subway: UrbanRail.net (www.urbanrail.net) publishes web links to subway maps in major cities worldwide, and Wikipedia has a comprehensive list as well as web links to subway maps. Also, google your location or check Google Maps to review a destination's subway map, if applicable. Many subway systems offer day passes and tourist passes that include unlimited train, bus, and subway travel.

Bus: For intercity bus service along established routes in a variety of countries, visit Busbud (www.busbud.com), which provides city-to-city bus schedules and tickets in more than eighty countries. Check out Routes International for a listing of metropolitan bus services.

Useful Travel Apps and Services

Apps are very convenient for travel and can assist with itinerary management as well as provide useful tools and services, such as alarm clocks, transportation routes, calculators, tipping advice, weather forecasts, maps and navigation, and translation. These tools and services can aid you in making certain aspects of travel easier, albeit fun.

Itinerary Management: I highly recommend TripIt (www.tripit.com), an itinerary-management app that conveniently organizes all of your travel bookings in one place by allowing you to forward your travel confirmation e-mails to TripIt's e-mail address. An added bonus is that TripIt will alert you to flight status changes.

Loyalty Program Apps: Most travel loyalty programs have apps (e.g., Marriott Mobile) that allow you to perform functions ranging from mobile check-in to online reservations. A related app, Stocard (www.stocardapp.com), helps you keep track of all of your loyalty program card information in one convenient place. It's useful for travel loyalty programs as well as nontravel loyalty programs.

Weather: Weather Underground (www.wunderground.com) is great because it allows you to see historical weather from the previous year, and I always review the weather from the prior year for my chosen dates to see what the actual weather conditions were. I also review Time and Date's (www.timeanddate.com) two-week extended forecast prior to taking any trips abroad.

Maps and Navigation: Mapping apps are very useful for helping you navigate your destination without necessarily needing cellular service. For example, with the Google Maps apps, you can download a city map for use offline or go to the Offline Areas within the app to add a destination. MapsMe (www.maps.me) and OsmAnd (www.osmand.net) are additional apps that perform similar functions.

Translation: Four great apps for translation are Google Translate, iTranslate Voice, Word Lens, and SpeechTrans. Google Translate is available in ninety languages and performs translations through typed words, text-to-audio translations, and spoken phrases. iTranslate Voice offers voice recognition translation in more than forty languages and allows responses in a foreign language to be translated into your native language. Word Lens, acquired by Google, allows you to aim your mobile phone at text and have it instantly translated on the screen in English, French, German, Italian, Portuguese, Russian, and Spanish without an Internet connection. For other languages, you can have text translated by taking a picture of the text first. SpeechTrans claims to offer the ability to have a complete conversation in any language. The company even has its own Bluetooth watch, which can be used to perform the translation functions, freeing you from holding your cell phone.

Photography: When I travel, I let my fingers do the snapping, since I never know what shot is going to turn out to be my masterpiece! If you aren't into taking tons of photos and want to try something different, Narrative Clip 2 (www.getnarrative.com) is a wearable camera that automatically snaps photos in intervals without your intervention, a very cool way to lessen the burden of taking a lot of pictures. While you won't have many pictures of yourself, you're sure to get numerous candid shots along the way. In addition, Flytographer (www.flytographer.com) will pair you with photographers for short on-location sessions in select destinations so you can focus on capturing iconic photos of your trip, while Postagram (www.sincerely.com/postagram) allows you to snap pictures with your phone and send printed postcards to your chosen recipients—a nice touch!

As for organizing trip photos, I create separate folders on my computer for each trip and subfolders within each trip folder for each location. Doing so makes finding my photos so easy, even when using highly recommended photo tools such as Google Photos, Dropbox, and the iCloud Photo Library. Dropbox can also be used to store travel documents online, such as copies of your passport. As for photography apps, try Fastcamera (iOS), Instagram, and Google Camera.

Dining and Restaurant Apps: The best websites or apps for locating and reviewing restaurants worldwide are:

- Foursquare (www.foursquare.com)
- OpenTable (www.opentable.com)
- TimeOut (www.timeout.com)
- TripAdvisor (www.tripadvisor.com)
- VegOut (www.vegoutapp.com)
- Yelp (www.yelp.com)
- Zagat (www.zagat.com)
- Zomato (www.zomato.com)

Exploring Another Culture

When you travel to a new destination, there are so many ways to experience it. You can take a slow pace or a fast pace. You can do activities on or off the beaten path. You can partake in popular culture and visit the well-known attractions or partake in lesser-known activities. When you follow a slower pace and are able to do as the locals do, you are more likely to gain a greater understanding of that location. I found this to be true when studying abroad in a country rather than visiting a country on vacation. However, there is no right or wrong way to approach this; you should do things that interest you in a manner that interests you, so long as the goal is cultural exploration. The key to quickly jumping into and understanding another culture depends on the place (how different the culture is from your own) and whether there is a language barrier. Below are six strategies for quickly immersing yourself in another culture:

1. Read about the destination. Prior to taking a vacation, I usually read a quick history of the place on Wikipedia. I also try to learn a few greetings if I am traveling to a country where I am not familiar with the language. Sawadee! Xièxie. I have found that many local people will embrace you if you try to adapt and respect their local customs.

2. Visit a museum. Museums are another avenue for learning about the history of a place. Art museums are a great way to do this and are especially good places to visit if the climate is cold. You might also learn something new, whether it's an artist you never heard of or a part of the country's history that is less well known.

3. Eat like a local. Don't go to Vietnam and eat at McDonald's! You would be missing out on one of the highlights of travel— food! Always keep an open mind, and eat only those foods you are comfortable eating. By trying something new, you might discover a new recipe you can try back home, or you might find that you never need to eat a certain food again. It's all a part of the adventure, right?

4. Attend a local event. Going to a national pastime event, concert, symphony, opera, local music festival, or other performance is a

great way to experience local culture and will provide insight into the destination. Just think about attending a Broadway show in New York City. Participating in a local event, such as Carnaval do Brasil in Rio, is even better. Some useful websites for researching events are Time Out (www.timeout.com), Ticketmaster (www.ticketmaster.com), Eventful (www.eventful.com), and Festivals 360 (www.festivals360.com).

5. Watch a foreign film. Though many Americans are not accustomed to reading subtitles, foreign films are an extraordinary way to gain insight into another culture. For the most authentic experience, choose a film that was produced in the country by local filmmakers. However, it is best to watch the foreign film before arriving in the country, because you don't want to lose valuable time exploring the destination and can watch a film anywhere, given today's technologies. Those long airplane flights often have a few great foreign films on demand.

6. Hire a local to show you around. If you have a friend living in the destination, you can gain all the immersion you need. However, if not, seeking tours by locals is a great way to learn a lot about a place and experience some off-the-beaten-path sites. A popular website for finding local tour guides is ToursByLocals (www.toursbylocals.com), and you can also opt for private tours through companies such as Viator (www.viator.com). Though tours are great for conveniently seeing the major attractions of a place when you have limited time to do so, I try to limit my involvement in large group tours, as they are usually impersonal and too rushed, leaving a lot of unanswered questions and no time to explore the sites visited.

Exploration and relaxation is the purpose of travel, and you can be assured to accomplish both by following the advice contained in step 5. The five key takeaways are as follows:

- Get ready for your trip using my twenty-step approach to trip preparation.
- Enroll in a trusted travel program such as Global Entry if you travel abroad more than once per year.

- Understand your cellular plan options overseas, and use Wi-Fi and apps to stay connected.
- Be careful about what you eat, get plenty of rest, and practice good hygiene.
- Learn as much as you can about your destination before your trip, and be receptive to and respectful of different customs and cultures.

CONCLUSION

Over the years, I have read a lot of health articles as well as self-help articles that have advocated finding one's purpose, and what I have concluded from consuming this information is that investing in all facets of your health, including the fourth dimension of health—vacationing—will help you grow as a person and strengthen your resolve to pursue your passions in life. I truly believe that the only thing preventing you from achieving a goal is the belief that you can't achieve it. So let today be the day you start believing that anything is possible.

Every journey begins with the first step, and your reading this book is a clear indication that you're ready to take the first step toward fulfilling your travel dreams. Not only is this pursuit worth your time, money, and effort, but it also provides the best souvenirs of all—memories. And my travel memories have made me happier than any possessions ever could, because, for me, travel is a voyage of self-discovery that forces us to enjoy the present, even if we're learning about the past. From my journeys around the world, I have been able to discover different cultures, languages, foods, music, arts, and ways of life. While uncovering the history of a place, I have actually been able to uncover something about myself, whether it's a hidden love of chocolate or a realization that no matter how many times I see the sun setting over the ocean, it never gets old.

In order to make your travel dreams come true, you must first have a plan, and even a short-term plan is a start. At the very minimum, you should invest time in figuring out specifically where you would like to go, and the more specific the plan, the easier it will be to figure out how to make it happen. In terms of funding your travel dreams, you should adopt at least one key travel-hacking strategy, such as obtaining at least one travel credit card on which you put all of your spending. And the more travel-hacking and -savings strategies you try, the more "capital" (i.e., miles, points, and money) you will be able to devote to your trip, thereby reducing your costs. Don't forget my other strategies to help you pack like a pro, fly with comfort and style, mitigate your travel risks, and hit the ground running at your destination of choice. So on your mark: mark your calendar with dates and destinations from your trip wish list. Get set: use the methodologies in this book to make preparing for travel a lot easier. Go: explore all that the world has to offer, and pursue a lifetime of travel. Bon voyage!

GLOSSARY

airline hub city: airports that an airline uses as a main base of operations to connect to destinations not served by direct flights

cash-back credit card: a card that provides a specified percentage of cash back, usually as a statement credit, for certain categories of purchases.

churning: continuously opening and closing credit card accounts for the purpose of obtaining sign-up bonuses

co-branded points: points earned with an airline- or hotel-branded credit card

fixed-value points: points that can be redeemed for a specific dollar amount of travel

fuel surcharge: a fee most commonly used by European and Asian airlines that was originally instituted to aid airlines in covering added expenses during periods when the cost of fuel is high

high season: the period of year when visitors and prices are highest

layover: time spent in a connection city between your originating city and destination

low season: the period of year when the fewest people visit a place, resulting in the lowest prices of the year loyalty program: a rewards program for frequent customers that typically offers discounts, special offers, rebates, prizes, or points

manufactured spending: the practice of making large purchases on credit cards for the purpose of earning travel rewards points, often while buying only cash equivalents that are used to repay the debt incurred

one-way: a flight itinerary that originates in one city and terminates in another city

open-jaw: a round-trip flight itinerary that either

> o originates in one city, terminates in a second city, and returns to the originating city from a third city (e.g., New York to Paris and London to New York on one round-trip ticket); or
> o originates in one city, terminates in a second city, and returns from the second city to a third city in the originating city's region (e.g., New York to Paris and Paris to Boston on one round-trip ticket)

region: an area designated by airlines for each destination, examples being North America and Europe

round-trip: a flight itinerary that returns to the city from which it originates

shoulder season: the period of year between low season and high season, when visitors and prices are neither the lowest nor the highest

stopover: a period of time longer than twenty-four hours deliberately spent in a connection city

transferable points: points that can be transferred to multiple loyalty programs

Appendix A:

OVERVIEW OF MAJOR US-BASED HOTEL PROGRAMS

There are nine major US-based hotel programs, each with its own loyalty program. All of these major hotel chains have co-branded credit cards that allow you to earn points toward free nights in addition to earning points from paid stays. In addition, most of these hotel chains are partners with a transferable points program, such as American Express Membership Rewards, and allow you to purchase gift cards, usually between $50 and $250 per gift card, using points for an average rate of about 12,000 points for $50. The following provides an overview of the major US-based hotel loyalty programs. Since this information is subject to change, please also consult each loyalty program's website.

Best Western

Best Western has more than 4,000 hotels in more than 100 countries across three brands: Best Western, Best Western Plus, and Best Western Premier. To obtain Best Western elite status, you would need to have 10, 15, or 30 qualifying nights or to have earned 10,000, 15,000, or 30,000 points to earn Gold, Platinum, or Diamond status, respectively. Hotel awards range from 8,000 points to 36,000 points per night. Best Western will match your elite status with any other hotel program via its Status Match No Catch program. Best Western is a transfer partner of Diners Club International. Best Western offers a few credit cards with sign-up bonuses ranging from 20,000 to 70,000 points, automatic Gold or Platinum status, and earning rates of $10 to $20 per dollar spent at Best Western properties. This brand caters mostly to domestic budget travelers in the United States, and there are not many luxury properties worldwide. The top-tier Best Western properties include Best Western Hotel Olimpia in Venice, Italy; Best Western Left Bank–St. Germain in Paris, France; Best Western Premier Louvre St. Honoré in Paris, France; Best Western Bangtao Beach Resort & Spa in Phuket, Thailand; Best Western Premier Hotel Royal Palace in Prague, Czech Republic; Best Western Premier Hotel Glockenhof in Zurich, Switzerland; and the Best Western Premier Terrace Hotel in Perth, Australia.

Choice Hotels

Choice Hotels is one of the world's largest hotel chains, boasting more than 6,000 properties across eleven brands. Choice Hotels is known as a budget hotel chain with brands including Comfort Inn and EconoLodge. Choice Privileges, the elite program, requires 10 nights for Gold status, 20 nights for Platinum status, and 40 nights for Diamond status. Award stays at Choice Hotels are not bookable very far in advance, as typically you can book no earlier than sixty days in advance, which is a stark contrast to other hotel brands, with which booking a year or more in advance is possible for general members. For paid stays, you will earn between 5 to 10 points per dollar spent at Choice properties. In addition, with the Choice Privileges Visa credit card, you will automatically receive Gold status, earn up to four free nights (depending on category of the hotel) for opening the account, and earn 15 points per dollar at Choice properties and 2 points per dollar on everyday purchases. Choice Hotels frequently offers promotions and status matches if you are an elite member of another hotel brand. Choice Hotels is a transfer partner of American Express Membership Rewards and Diners Club International. In addition, you can transfer Amtrak points into Choice points at a ratio of 1:3, which means that 1,000 Amtrak points become 3,000 Choice points. The best benefit of Choice Hotels is its partnership with the Preferred Hotel & Resorts Group, wherein you can redeem Choice points at more than 100 luxurious Preferred Hotels properties around the world. The caveat is that award nights can be booked only within thirty days of arrival. The Preferred Hotels & Resort properties represent the top-tier hotels bookable through the Choice Hotels program. Such properties are too numerous to name but include the Alchymist Grand Hotel & Spa in Prague, Czech Republic; Peter Island Resort & Spa in the British Virgin Islands; Es Saadi Palace in Marrakech, Morocco; the NH Collection Venezia Palazzo Barocci; and the Jefferson Hotel in Washington, DC.

Club Carlson

With more than 1,000 hotels across six brands, including the Radisson, Radisson Blu, Quorvus Collection, Park Plaza, Country Inn & Suites, and Park Inn, Club Carlson is what I would call a midtier hotel program, as its hotels tend not to be of the same standard as Marriott, Hilton, or Starwood. Earning points is relatively easy, as you earn 20 Gold Points per dollar spent at hotels, independently of owning their credit card. With the Club Carlson Premier Rewards and Business Rewards Visa cards, you automatically receive Gold Elite status, which provides an additional 35 percent bonus on points earned at hotels. In addition, signing up for one of these cards yields 85,000 points as a sign-up bonus after meeting minimum spending requirements. Club Carlson offers arguably the easiest way to get a free night, since free nights start at 9,000 points. Club Carlson also has some great promotions, which can provide even greater points earning. However, there is no complimentary breakfast. Club Carlson's top properties, which are 70,000 points per night, are the Mayfair in London, the Radisson Royal Hotel in Moscow, and four Radisson Blu hotels in France.

Hilton Hotels

With nearly 4,000 hotels across ten brands worldwide, Hilton definitely has a broad reach, and there are a multitude of methods to earn Hilton HHonors points. For one, there are at least fifteen different credit cards that earn up to 10 Hilton HHonors points per dollar spent at Hilton hotels and between 3 to 6 points on other purchases, depending on the spending category. American Express Membership Rewards points also transfer at 1:1.5 to Hilton, while Diners Club International points transfer at 1:1.6 to Hilton. Some credit cards, such as the Citi Hilton HHonors Reserve card, provide Gold status and the option to attain Diamond status when spending $40,000 in purchases each year.

With Gold status, free breakfast, free Internet, room upgrades, and late checkout are offered. Hilton offers the fifth night free for every four nights booked, and hotel awards range from 5,000 to 95,000 points. Top-tier Hilton properties are the Conrad Maldives and Hilton Bora Bora at 95,000 points per night, the Conrad Koh Samui, and two Hilton-brand hotels in the Seychelles.

Hyatt Hotels

With nearly 600 hundred hotels across eleven brands, Hyatt has one of the smaller portfolios of US-based hotel chains. Overall, Hyatt Gold Passport is a great rewards program, though earning points is not very easy because Hyatt has fewer hotels than other chains and its hotels are concentrated in major cities in the United States, Europe, and Asia. However, elite status is relatively easy to attain with Hyatt. For example, you can earn Platinum status with just 5 stays or 15 nights; and Diamond status with only 25 stays or 50 nights, which is far fewer stays or nights than most competitors require (usually 75 nights). Hyatt offers free breakfast for Diamond status members, and nights paid for with cash plus points count toward elite status. Award nights for standard rooms range from 5,000 to 30,000 points per night. However, you can use points to book suites or to upgrade a paid stay to a suite. This is fantastic, considering that you cannot book an upgraded room with most other hotel chains for a reasonable number of points, if at all, and you usually have to pay cash for upgrades. Hyatt is a transfer partner of Chase Ultimate Rewards and Diners Club International and has its own co-branded credit cards. When you enroll in Hyatt's Gold Passport program, you receive Gold status, which is akin to general membership in other brands and earns 5 base points per dollar spent at Hyatt properties. The Hyatt Visa credit card automatically comes with Platinum status and one free night in a category 1 to 4 hotel every year that you maintain the card. In addition, the sign-up bonus for this card is two free nights at any Hyatt property after spending $1,000 in the first three months after the account is opened. This means you can spend two free nights at Hyatt's top properties, which are the Park Hyatt Maldives, the Park Hyatt Paris-Vendome, and the Park Hyatt Sydney.

InterContinental Hotels

With more than 4,500 hotels worldwide, InterContinental Hotels (IHG) has a variety of hotel brands, which include Holiday Inn, Crowne Plaza, Hotel Indigo, and InterContinental. IHG's elite status has three tiers: Gold, Platinum, and Spire. One of the selling points of IHG's rewards program is its promotions, such as Into the Nights, discount awards, and Points Breaks, which offers promotional award stays of 5,000 points per night at select hotels. The IHG Visa is one of the best values among hotel credit cards because of its high sign-up bonus (between 70,000 and 80,000 points) and because it offers a free night at any IHG hotel for every year you have the card. In addition, with the card, you will receive a 10 percent rebate of the points redeemed for hotel awards. IHG is a transfer partner of Chase Ultimate Rewards and Diners Club International. IHG's top-tier properties are the InterContinental London Westminster, InterContinental London Park Lane, InterContinental Paris Le Grand, InterContinental Bora Bora Resort & Thalasso, InterContinental Le Moana Bora Bora, and InterContinental Resort & Spa Moorea. And at the InterContinental properties in Bora Bora, you can book an overwater villa at the standard rate of 50,000 points per night, which is not possible with Hilton or Starwood.

Marriott Hotels

With more than 4,000 hotels across fifteen brands, Marriott offers a wide spectrum of hotels, including Ritz Carlton, Autograph Collection, and Protea Hotels, and has a wealth of properties in Spain, the Caribbean, Hawaii, and Asia. With the Marriott Rewards Premier Visa credit card, you earn 50,000 points after spending $1,000 in the first three months after the account is opened, and you receive fifteen nights' credit toward elite status, which is enough for Silver status. Even though, the credit card provides a free night at a category 1 to 4 hotel for every year of card membership, there are really no great hotels in this category, because the brand has consistently raised the category level of its properties. Most category 1 to 4 hotels are Fairfield Inns, Courtyard by Marriott hotels, or domestic properties. For its top-tier properties, Marriott charges 45,000 points per night at category 9 properties and 70,000 points per night at Tier 5 Ritz-Carlton properties. Gold status provides free Wi-Fi, free breakfast, room upgrades, and late checkout, and when you redeem four nights, the fifth night is free. The best use of Marriott points is for air-and-hotel travel packages. For between 200,000 and 540,000 Marriott points, you get seven nights in a resort plus between 35,000 to 132,000 airline miles, depending on the category of the hotel you select. Though it will take some effort to get this many points, it's a great deal because seven nights at a Ritz Carlton Tier 5 property is 490,000 points alone. Thus, for only 50,000 additional Marriott points, you could receive 132,000 United airline miles, a nearly 1:3 conversion to valuable airline miles. Marriott is a transfer partner of Chase Ultimate Rewards and Diners Club International. Top-tier Marriott properties are the Ritz-Carlton and Autograph properties. Among the brand's best properties are the Ritz-Carlton hotels in London, Ritz-Carlton Montreal, Ritz-Carlton Grand Cayman, Boscolo Exedra Roma, and the Boscolo Budapest. Ritz-Carlton also has Ritz-Carlton Reserve hotels, which are even more exclusive properties.

<u>Starwood Hotels</u>

Starwood Hotels offers some of the best hotels in the world, and though they only have 1,200 properties in 100 countries across nine brands, they have luxurious properties in some of the world's most coveted and exotic destinations, including French Polynesia, the Greek Isles, Thailand, and Italy. The problem with Starwood is that points are hard to earn unless you are a frequent business traveler, which is probably what the brand prefers. The Starwood American Express card certainly helps, but it earns only 1 point per dollar spent, whereas most other credit cards earn multiple points per dollar spent. Starwood is also a transfer partner of Diners Club International, but the transfer ratio is less than 1:1. Therefore, it will take a lot of spending to earn a free night at a top-tier Starwood property, regardless of how you earn points. Starwood offers the fifth night free for award bookings at category 3 or higher properties, and the American Express Platinum card offers Starwood Gold Elite status along with many other benefits to justify its $450 annual fee. With Starwood, you will also retain Platinum status after staying 500 nights or maintaining Platinum status for ten years.

Though there are some spectacular properties, it is likely better to redeem Starpoints at lower-tier properties, such as the Meridien Siem Reap; to use cash-and-points redemptions; or to convert points to airline miles with more than thirty airlines. Airline transfers are perhaps the best benefit of the program, and if you transfer Starpoints in increments of 20,000, you receive a 5,000-point bonus in airline miles. Though earning points would require a lot of effort, there are many top-tier Starwood properties, including the St. Regis Bora Bora; Prince de Galles, in Paris; Blue Palace, in Crete; the St. Regis Florence; Vana Belle, in Koh Samui; W South Beach; Al Maha, in Dubai; W Retreat, in Maldives; Tambo del Inka, in Peru; and the St. Regis Bali.

Wyndham

With nearly 8,000 properties in seventy countries across fifteen brands, Wyndham is the world's largest hotel chain. Wyndham is definitely a budget-friendly chain with brands that include Days Inn, Ramada, Super 8, Travelodge, and Howard Johnson. Wyndham's loyalty program, Wyndham Rewards, offers a flat redemption rate of 15,000 points per night at all Wyndham hotels. By being a member of Wyndham Rewards, you earn 10 points per dollar spent at Wyndham hotels. In addition, Wyndham has two visa credit cards: a no-fee version and an annual-fee version. With the no-fee version, you earn 12,000 points after your first purchase, 3 points per dollar spent at Wyndham properties, and 2 points per dollar spent everywhere else. With the sixty-nine-dollar-annual-fee version, you earn 30,000 points after your first purchase (enough for two nights at any Wyndham), 5 points per dollar spent at Wyndham properties, 2 points per dollar spent everywhere else; and 5,500 points on your account anniversary each year. You can achieve Wyndham Gold status with twenty qualifying nights in a calendar year, and you will be rewarded automatically with 15,000 Gold status points (different from regular rewards points) just for reaching Gold status. Gold status points enable you to book Go Free awards within four months of receiving the Gold status points and Go Fast awards, which allow you to book a hotel room for 3,000 points per night plus cash. Other than that, there are no real advantages to having Wyndham Gold status, so the program falls short of other loyalty programs by not offering additional elite perks, such as free Wi-Fi, late checkout, and free breakfast, although some of

Wyndham's hotel brands offer free breakfast to all guests. Wyndham's top-tier properties include the Shelborne Wyndham Grand South Beach; Wyndham Guayaquil; Silverado Resort, in Napa, California; and Le Moulin de Vernègues, in Provence, France.

***

In summary, there are a variety of US-based hotel programs and a variety of ways to earn and use hotel points. For example, many hotel programs allow conversions into airline miles (generally not recommended) or double-dipping with airline programs. In addition, Best Western, Club Carlson, Hyatt, Marriott, and Starwood allow you to pool or transfer points to friends or family, so points can be combined for an award. IHG and Hilton charge a fee for doing so, while Choice Hotels and Wyndham do not allow transfers to anyone else.

Appendix B:

OVERVIEW OF AMTRAK GUEST REWARDS PROGRAM

Amtrak Guest Rewards offers 2 points for every dollar spent on Amtrak and 500 points for every qualifying Acela Business Class trip. Redemptions start at only 1,500 points, and there are four classes of service: Coach, Business, Roomette, and Bedroom. Roomettes accommodate two people, while Bedrooms accommodate three people, and both classes provide meals. Amtrak has four zones: Western, Central, Eastern, and Northeastern, the latter being a subset of the Eastern zone. To travel from Washington, DC, to Montreal, Canada, which is the Northeastern zone, would cost 4,000 points in Coach, 6,500 points in Business, 15,000 points for a Roomette, and 20,000 points for a Bedroom. For travel solely within the other zones, the rates are 5,500 points in Coach, 6,500 in Business, 15,000 points for a Roomette, and 25,000 points for a Bedroom. Rates are higher for trips that cover multiple zones. Additional rate details are located on Amtrak's Guest Rewards page. Amtrak allows members to share points with friends and family. For trips across the United States as well as travel with a family, using points for Amtrak awards would be a super cool way to travel.

Amtrak is a transfer partner of Chase Ultimate Rewards and Diners Club International. Other ways to earn and use Amtrak points are via rental-car companies and hotel chains. When you rent a car with Budget, Enterprise, or Hertz, you can earn 50 Amtrak Guest Rewards points for every qualifying rental day. Amtrak also allows members to transfer points to two hotel programs: Hilton and Choice. When transferred, 5,000 Amtrak points becomes 10,000 Hilton HHonors points and 15,000 Choice Privileges points. Of the two hotel transfer options, Choice Privileges is the better option, given Choice's partnership with the Preferred Hotel Group. In order to be eligible to transfer Amtrak points to hotel partners, you must spend $200 on the Amtrak Guest Rewards MasterCard, which is no longer being offered to new customers, or obtain Amtrak elite status, which requires earning a minimum of 5,000 qualifying points on Amtrak. You can transfer up to 25,000 Amtrak points per calendar year, which would equate to 75,000 Choice points.

DISCLAIMER

The information contained in this book is meant to serve as a comprehensive guide to travel. Therefore, strategies and tips are only recommendations, and reading this book does not guarantee specific or intended results. I have made all reasonable efforts to provide current and accurate information for the readers of this book and will not be held liable for any unintentional errors or omissions that may be found.

The material in this book may include information or links of third parties. Third-party materials comprise the products and opinions expressed by their owners. As such, this book does not assume responsibility or liability for any third-party materials or opinions. The publication of such third-party materials does not constitute my guarantee of any information, instruction, opinion, products, or service contained within the third-party material or website. Use of recommended third-party material does not guarantee that your results will mirror mine. Publication of such third-party material is simply a recommendation and expression of my own opinion of that material.

Whether because of the general evolution of the Internet, or the unforeseen changes in company policy and editorial submission guidelines, what is stated as fact at the time of this writing, may become outdated or simply inapplicable at a later date. This may also apply to the various companies that I have referenced in this book.

No part of this publication shall be reproduced, transmitted, or resold in whole or in part in any form, without prior written consent.

INDEX